Jacaranda

Jacaranda

Waiting for Love in Forlornness

蓝花楹 - 在绝望中等待爱情

Zhao Crowley

向 昭

Library of Congress Control Number: 2018904403
ISBN: Hardcover   978-1-5434-0850-8
                 Softcover   978-1-5434-0849-2
                 eBook   978-1-5434-0848-5

摄影师：戴璐
Photographer: Ms. Lydia Dai

封面肖像：陈雪樵
Cover Model: Ms. Jodie Chen

Print information available on the last page.

Rev. date: 04/27/2018

To order additional copies of this book, contact:
Xlibris
1-800-455-039
www.Xlibris.com.au
Orders@Xlibris.com.au
773815

CONTENTS

蓝花楹
—— 在绝望中等待爱情

JACARANDA

– Waiting for love in forlornness

For the purpose of keeping freedom of the spirit in the material world, I wrote these poems.

在物质的世界里，保持一份精神的自由，是我写诗的目的

《夜》
NIGHT

夜

Night

是谁的忧伤

Whose blueness it was

漆黑了你的面庞

That darkened your face

没有一丝星光

There is even no piece of light coming from stars

念

Miss

或如一把利剑

May, like a sharp sword

刺痛无尽的苍穹

Break through the indefinite sky

寻找归依的地方

Looking for a relegation place

无知无觉

Unconsciously no feelings, no sense

破晓了天光

The twilight breaks through

又是蒙面于琐碎

Masks self into the trivial again

隐没于凡世的来来往往

Disappears into the ordinary life, come and go

《迷失》
LOST

穿林越路

Pass through the forest / Go over the road

迷失在这条花径

Lost in this flower palace

芬芳馥郁

Fragrant fragrance

却难追寻蝶的踪迹

But, it's difficult to follow butterflies' trail

是谁

Who it is

撩拨了灵魂的梦息

Luring a dream from my soul

从沉睡中苏醒

Wake me up from the deep sleep

遥叹难及的幸福

Sigh the sigh of pursuing a dizzy happiness

沉沦于枯寂的囹圄

Locked in the lonesome shackles

忽而天光云影

Suddenly break the shadow of clouds

籍天使的翅膀

Revive angel's wings

重振裂勇

Retrive the braveness

带我飞翔

Taking me to fly

去那渴望的心乡

To the desired home of my heart

《拥抱》
HUG

小时候

In my childhood

妈妈的拥抱

The hug from Mum

是一种温暖

Is kind of warm

满布的芳香

Full of sweetness

稳稳的心安

Stabilizing relief

那就是家

It is a feeling of home

长大了

When growing up

一个人的漂泊

I led a wandering life by myself

为着所谓的辉煌

For the purpose of pursuing so-called glorious

却丢失了拥抱

As a result – I, lost hugs

把自己孤单成一匹骆驼

Lonely/ Like a camel

在沙漠中负重跋涉

I trudge in the desert/ bearing a heavy burden

带起了面具

Put on masks, and

掩藏了真心

Hide a true heart

人前桃花春风面

Peach-blossom face with spring smiles in front of people

哪知潇潇弱水寒

However/ who knows the tears and sadness when you were alone

不觉时光碾转

Unconscious of the flying of time

就沧桑了心情

The heart has vicissitudes

花白了发鬓

White climbs into hairs

仍然寻觅

Still searching for

一份温暖的拥抱

A hug with warmness

入梦入心

In the dream / In the heart

回到从前

Went back to my childhood

稳稳的安

Stabilizing relief returns

《蓝花楹的倒下》[1]
THE FALLEN JACARANDA

花开考试来

Blossoming/ Jacaranda brings examination time

花落考试过

Dropping off flowers / Passed the test

你把自己绚烂的紫

Jacaranda holds her gorgeous purple color

站成一树期盼的景

Standing herself into a view with whole tree's hope

风里、雨里陪伴

Accompany / No fear of wind or rain

以为可以永恒

Believing /It could become a forever

却也逃不过最终的劫

Yet/ Unable to escape the final catastrophe

倒下

Fallen/ The jacaranda tree

仍然骄傲

Still holds tightly of its pride

撒播一地的厚重

Spreading thick all over the earth

8

花飞花散

Flowers flying/ Flowers scattering

云卷云舒

Clouds curling /Clouds stretching

换成一世的怀念

Exchanging the yearning of a livelihood

染透心紫的永恒

Dye the forever purple of heart

《牧马人》
WRANGLER

一匹马

A horse

一个人

A man

一堆篝火

A bonfire

心中的海子

Hai Zi[2] in the heart

面朝大海

Facing the sea

春暖花开

Spring warm brings blossom of flowers

幸福可以很简单

Happiness could be a simple thing

纯粹的心境

Pure mind

不屈于磨折的骄傲

Unyielding pride

望天天高

Watching sky and sky high

眺海海阔

Watching sea and sea broad

翻山越岭

Over mountains and cross hills

泥湿了双脚

Feet wet

仍守于初心

Still, kept a heart of beginning

骑士之仪

Knight manner

王者风

Demeanor of KING

《欲望的都市》

CITY OF DESIRES

欲望的都市

City of desires

钢筋水泥下压抑的灵魂

Souls under reinforced concrete

行走在车水马龙的繁华中

Walking among bustling vehicles and people

寻求，迷惘，不知所措

Seek, confused, overwhelmed

麻木在

Numbness

无爱失痛的沼泽里

In the swamp, unable to feel love or pain

醉也未解千愁

Unable to resolve thousands of worries, even while drunk

逃离、逃离、逃离

Escaping, Escaping, Escaping

绝望主妇

Desperate housewives

欲望都市里的女子们

Ladies in the city of desires

寻找一片净土

Seeking a piece of pure land

有着蓝的天空, 白的云彩

With blue skies, white clouds

一路而北

All the way towards the north

心向往之的炫紫

To the gorgeous purple, for the desires of heart

慢的节奏

Slow down the rhythm

模糊了现实的苟且

Muddle along the reality

有诗和远方的田野

Get to the distant field of poems

沉落的夕阳

Sunset sinking

满落绯红的池塘

Crimson falling into the pond

悠长的牧牛哞鸣

Long pasture chimes and cattle eating grass

一段枯木苍穹

A long-dead wood,

天空之城的歌声

Song from the city of sky above

四颗纯粹的心灵

Four pure hearts

女人们的友情

Friendships of ladies

纯净在乡村的田野里

Purified by the stunning country view

忘掉吧，欲望的都市

Let's forget-the city of desires

Photo by: Jodie Chen   摄影：陈雪樵

Model: Zhao Crowley （Left Front)   人物：向昭 （左前）

Lydia Dai (Left Back)   戴璐 （左后）

Selina Luo (Right Back)   罗景泊 （右后）

《九宫格人生》
LIFE IN NINE STYLISH LATTICES

上帝关上了一扇门

God closed a door

请你相信

Please be in faith

他关掉的是一室的黑暗

It was the darkness of the room that he closed

也请你静心的等候

Please be quiet and wait

必有一扇窗将为你打开

There will be a window to be opened for you

那一窗里

Through that window

将有满布的阳光

Full sunlight will enter

充盈的温暖

Full of warmth

因为你是上帝的孩子

Because you are the child of God

为了完成一个完美的塑造

He wants to complete a masterpiece of art, and

16

雕刻的疼痛也会跟随

You may feel pain in the process of being completed

如果你想

If you want

有一个九宫格的人生

To have a life in nine stylish lattice

每一格里都有不同的精彩

To have unique excellence in each lattice

每一格里都有不同的姿态

To have a stylish posture in every lattice

每一格的姿态都有你悉心的经营

Each stylish posture has the full care of your management

那就请你

Then please

别怕雕琢的痛

Don't be afraid of the pain from completion

用你最美的微笑面对所有

Face all these pains with the most beautiful smile

Photo by: Lydia Dai　　摄影：戴璐

Model: Zhao Crowley　　人物：向昭

《水墨庄园》
INKY FAIRY LIGHT MANOR

在那诗和远方

In that poetic remote area

有一座水墨庄园

There is an inky manor

在那日出前的早晨

In the morning before the sun rise

你会迷失在氤氲的雾气中

You could be lost in the mixing fog

象是走进了中国水墨画

Seems that you walked into a traditional Chinese picture

我们给她取了个美丽的名字

We give the manor a beautiful name--

叫做Fairylight--仙灯庄园

It's called Fairy light Manor

我曾和我的闺蜜

I and with my girlfriends

在这里寻找心灵的方向

Came here to find a direction for our souls

我们的笑声如瀑布

Our laughing sounds like waterfalls

我们的脚步轻灵地穿过田野

We cross over the field with brisk steps

田野中有牧牛

In the field there are cattle

跳跃的袋鼠

Kangaroos jumping freely

和唱歌的小鸟

With birds singing happily

我们追寻着太阳的方向

We run towards the sun

把心中的雾霾驱散

Getting the haze out of our hearts

当金光跃上高空

When the golden sunshine rises in the sky

树枝上的叶涤荡了露水

Leaves of branches wash away dew

玫瑰的芬芳就会洒满心房

Rose fragrance fully fills our hearts

庄园里住着归隐的帕玛老太

Lady elder Pam hermits in the manor

她游历过世界，

She ever traveled around the world

洞悉过人心，

She insights hearts of people

历尽了磨难

She experienced suffers

故事写满参天松柏的年轮

Her stories were written into the rings of a pine tree

一圈一圈四十二载

One after one, total 42 rings

从帕玛老太的亲手种植

The stories started from the year she planted the pine tree

写到克莱润斯河的血色黄昏

To the current time when bloody evening of sunset spreads over the clearance river

绯红的河水倒映着天空之城

Crimson river water reflected the city shadow of the sky

心灵的修炼就在这水墨的庄园

It is this inky manor that brings four hearts cultivation

我们匆匆复匆匆地在凡世里追寻

We pursue restless over and over in this plain world

直到生命将尽的终点才来回归

Until close to the end of life, then, we return

返璞归真与自然亲近

Back to basics, close to nature

源于宇宙归于泥土

Comes from the universe, returns back to the earth

简简单单最是真

Then we know-the simplest is the best and true

Photo By: Selina Luo   摄影：罗景泊

Model: Zhao Crowley (Left)   人物：向昭（左）

　　　Lydia Dai (Right)   戴璐（右）

　　　Jodie Chen (Middle)   陈雪樵（中）

《各自为营》
SELF CAMP ON EACH SIDE

你是山，山巅入云

You are the mountain, summit reaches clouds

我是水，奔腾入海

I am water, running towards the sea

路不相同，各自为营

We have different path, we self-camp on our own side

却也相依，穿峡越谷

But, we stand by each other, crossing over valleys, surpassing through gorges

山不懂水的柔

Yet, mountain doesn't know the soft of water

水不解山的硬

Water doesn't understand the hard of mountain

山映水中央

Mountain reflects into water

水滴山石穿

Water drops wear through mountain rocks

相融相化

Try to assimilated each other

抑或渐行渐远

Or we may depart further and further

水始终在路上

Water runs her way all the time

不会停留

Never stop

直到山的靠近

Until the approach by mountain

走向现实

Winding each other to the reality

走向那个踢不烂的梦想

Walking towards to that dream which cannot be broken

或许时间是答案

Only time has the answer

Photo by: Zhao Crowley　　　摄影：向昭

《看月》
APPRECIATE MOON

我在海边看月

I am appreciating the moon alongside a sea

海风轻拂

Wind from the sea touches my face softly

吹散翯翯长发

And, breezes up my hair gently

潮起潮落

Tides rise up and tides withdraw back

打湿一心微浪

Wetting small waves in my heart

看月升月圆

The moon rises up and rounds itself slowly

云遮云散

Clouds covers, clouds scatters

缘来或缘去

Doom comes and goes

此事古难全

This is hard to be fulfilled from the world beginning

只把等待化沙尘

Melt the wait into sands

扬手撒入海

Throw the sands into the sea

抬头望

Raising head and looking up

一点星辰伴月色

Twinkle star appears beside the moon

守得云开见月明

And moonlights broke through the scattered clouds

明月光辉入海水

Spreading silvers on surface of seawater

万家灯火次第亮

One after one, home lights lighting up

一个字的温暖就是家

"HOME" is the word for warm

《尘埃之花》
FLOWER OF DUST

尘埃之花

Flower of dust

用微弱的自尊

Holding a weak dignity

支撑着脚步

Firming its foot

绝尘而去

Pull away

我听见

I heard

花瓣跌落的声音

The sound of falling from petals

纵使一片片化进泥土

Piece by piece, melted into earth

力量的轻薄

Weak strength

而至无声无息

Makes it hard to be heard and silence kept

夜色茫茫

Vast night

望不见你的面庞

I could not see your face

只有星辰闪烁

Only stars shinning

在路灯的昏暗里

In the dim of road lights

拉长你的影

Your shadow was stretched

决绝淡漠

Exclusive and Indifferent

花瓣飞扬跌落

Petals flying, Petals falling

夏夜的尘埃

Dust in this summer night

也有温度

Has temperature

灼伤的痛该如何治愈

How do petals cure pains burned by loveless

《时光隧道》
TIME CHANNEL

我站在时光的隧道里

Standing in the time channel

看着从前

Looking back to the past

那里有你有我

You and me were there

还有初次的相遇

With our first met

我看见一个温暖的面庞

I saw a warm face

带着孩子的纯真

With child's innocent

却也挥洒着艺术家的不羁

Yet also sway unruly of artist

心中有一方黑暗被亮光击中

A block of darkness deep inside was hit by light

但我并不知道这亮光的名字

But I don't know the name of this light

以后的时光里

The past travels in the channel

有骏马嘶鸣

There were neighing of horses

黑白色跳跃的身影

A black and white figure jumping

以及篮球架上方的天空

I saw sky above the basketball hoop

天空蓝的耀眼明亮

Blue sky bright and shine

让我想再挂上一道彩虹

I long to hang up a rainbow

彩虹之上便是那七彩的温柔

Above the rainbow, it is seven-color tenderness

心在这温柔中融化

It is the heart that melted in this tenderness

但我不知道这温柔也有名字

Neither, I don't know, there was a name for this tender

亮光与温柔在心间滋长

Light and tender grow in my heart

时光不停留

Time never stops

你时而热情时而冷漠

You are, sometimes enthusiasm, sometime indifferent

在时光的隧道里玩闹

Playing in the time channel

我却象个无助的孩子

But, feel so helpless, I am, like a baby

抵不过亮光的炫目

Unable to resist the drizzling of the light

温柔的虐心

Neither the heart bluely from tender

甘心在时光的隧道里追随

Willing to follow in the time channel

是的

YES

还有音乐，画布与诗歌

There were music, canvas and poems

我们或许巧遇或许相约

We may encounter by chance, or, may meet by arrange

并肩在时光的隧道里

Stood in the time channel, shoulder by shoulder

把这亮光尽情的挥洒

Spreading the light, filling the heart with full enjoyable

或许灼伤了别人的眼睛

It may burn the eyes of others

那又何妨

What does that a matter?

光阴的故事里为何不能任性

Why could not we throw the capricious into the story of time

或许是这亮光太亮

The light may be too bright

有时也会灼伤自己

Sometimes it burns us

痛彻心扉却也无法放开的温柔

Although pains cross through the whole heart, yet could not let the
tender go

如飞蛾扑火

Like a moth throw itself into fire

只是向往着那道光明

It was the brightness that it chases for

带我去到一个温暖的地方

Hoping to be taken to a place full of warm

于是我仍然执着

Persistence, I keep on going,

执着在时光隧道的穿梭里

Persistent in shuttling-commute in the time tunnel

《猫》
A CAT

恍如梦里来

Trance, woke up from a dream

又见喵星人

I saw a cat

夜色下软萌的身躯

Soft body in the light of night

措不及防地掀开尘封的往昔

Sealed memories suddenly returns

三十几载的光阴

Thirty years time

仍然不能忘却

Still could not forget

最初的宠爱

The first pet I have had

就是灯光闪耀下的白色小猫

It was a white fluffy cat

神气活现地走在书桌上

That wondering under my table lamp, lively on my desk

一直走在心里三十年

Since then, she wondered in my heart for over thirty years

换成心底最柔软的念

Became the forever softest miss in my heart

想拥入怀中

Long to pull her into my hug again

再感受一下傲娇的姿态

Feel its pride, feel its soft

就差　秒的冲动

Almost in a second

会夺步而前

I rushed up to hold it agin

阿库呐玛塔塔

A Ku Na Ma Ta Ta

《冰火两重天》

A TALE OF ICE AND FIRE

你就是南极大陆的一缕阳光

It is you who are sunlights of the Antarctica,

即使温度曾经炙热

Although ever have been hot

也难耐冰封万年的寒冷

Yet unable to tolerant the cold from millions of years ago

或许装傻是一种境界

Pretend being fool may be a realm

换来一份优雅的转身

For exchanging an elegant turn

有尊严的退出

Leave with dignity

只有那邂逅的爱情

However, the love encountered

仍然执着于心底

Still alive, persistently sink into the deep of the heart

哭泣着慢慢褪去的温度

Crying for the slowly cooling down temperature

我将这份温度攒成尖厉的冰川

Hold this temperature, I freeze it to a sharp glacier

透明晶莹，立于雪山之巅

Transparent crystal, standing on top of Snow Mountain

祭奠世事无常

Memorial the impermanent of the world

从此收起我的奢望

Hide away my luxury hope from now on

你在夏天

You stay in Sumer

我仍是冬天的摩羯

I am still that Capricorn of winter

冰火两重天

A tale of ice and fire

人生若只如初见……

Story the legend of the first met

《擦肩而过》
RUSHING BY

茫茫人海

Vast world, full of people

有多少机率可以重逢

How many chances there are for meeting again

擦肩而过

Rushing by

却忘记该怎样回眸一笑

But forgot to look back with smiles

你在彼岸望着天

Watching sky, you were on the other side

我在原点望着地

Eyeing land, I was on this side

或许你看不到忐忑的心

Perturbed heart, you are unable to see

也或许我选择刻意的茫然

At a loss on purpose, it was a choice that I made

终于还是喊不出口

Swallowed in mouth, calling wasn't out

擦肩而过

Rushing by

各自走在各自的轨道上

We walk on our own ways

《大海*美人鱼》

SEA AND MERMAID

--写给安徒生童话中的美人鱼

----------for the Anderson's fairy tale 《Mermaid》

你说你喜欢看大海

You said, watching sea is what you like

在你难过的时候

At the time when you feel sad

可能是因为

It may because that, when

惊涛拍岸

Storms beat shores

让你有一种英雄气概

Hero spirit touches you

疗却你内心的伤痛

It cures your pain from your heart

云高海阔

Clouds high, Sea broad

不再为俗琐而累

Pulling away tiredness of trivial

我想我是一尾美人鱼

I think I am a mermaid

住在海底王宫

Lingering in the King Palace at the bottom of the sea

无风无浪的深海

No storm no waves in the quiet depth

我只想做　个

I only want to be--

礼仪规范的公主

A princess obeys sea kingdom rules

然而海巫的魔镜

Unfortunately, I looked through a magic mirror of a sea wizard

让我看到了英雄气概的王子

I saw you, a prince with hero spirit

我服下海巫的炼丹

I swallowed alchemy of the sea wizard

把鱼尾剪成了双脚

And cut fish tail into foot

只为能浮出深海

Only wish that I could float out of the sea

走在路上与你相遇

Walking on the road to meet you

坐在海边的你

Sitting onshore beside the sea

面容俊朗却忧郁

Your handsome face is grim

看着大海浪涛相连

Watching waves claping one after one

服下海巫药丸的我

Swallowed alchemy of the sea wizard

出卖了声音

I sold my voice for this exchange

而无法说出爱恋

I am unable to speak out of my love

海巫说

Sea wizard says

得不到爱情的美人鱼

A mermaid who cannot get her beloved

死去后不会有灵魂

She will no longer has her soul after the death

只会幻化成海浪上的碎沫

Only, she will become foams floating above waves

一波波的冲击海岸线

Impacting sea shore with waves after waves

鱼尾剪成的双脚

Foot cut from fish tail

踩在路上每一步都是痛

Walking on the road with pains at each step

靠近你的路是那么的遥远

It is so far to be near you

我怕我等不到那天

I am afraid that I could not wait until the day

就会幻化成白浪的泡沫

I would have already became foams of white waves

只愿随波逐流

Drifting, drifting and drifting with waves

被你看到

Only wish to be seen by you

抹平愈合你心底的伤

And wave away the hurt from the bottom of your heart

Photo by: Zhao Crowley   摄影：向昭

《自画像》
SELF PORTRAIT

热闹的时候

At a jolly time

突然就会偶遇疏离

Alienated could suddenly break through

把自己变成一只鸵鸟

I made myself become as an ostrich

头埋进沙土

Hiding my head into sands

只留一丝呼吸的空间

Only keep a slot to breath

朋友说我是一个奇怪的人

I am a strange person, friends said

热情的时候象火

I am fire when I am enthusiasm

可以燃尽整个森林

Could burn a whole forest

冰冷的时候象雪山

I am a snow mountain when I am indifferent

冰冻万年的寒

Hold million years' cold inside

我只想说

But, I just want to say

其实我不想被稻草压垮

Because I don't want to be crushed by straws

才把自己隔在围墙之外

I isolated myself outside of the wall

听这世界的喧喧闹闹

Listening noisy of the world

也看看蓝天白云的清高

Watching clear high clouds on sky

没有呼吸陪伴的时候

When no accompany of respiration

就自己修炼孤独

I practice loneliness to bc myself

修成一身的坚壳

Transforming a hard shell cover my whole body

遇热而滚烫

Became hot when encounter enthusiasm

遇冷则冰凉

Became cold when facing indifference

其实壳下只留一颗软心

Actually, there is a soft heart kept underneath

夜深人静的时候

In tranquil dark deep nights

数数遥远的星辰

Counting remote stars

壳下的心寄托给最亮的那颗

Entrusting my heart under the shell to the brightest star

Photo by: Selina Luo　摄影：罗景泊

Model: Zhao Crowley　人物：向昭

《感恩》
THANKSGIVING

因为有你

Because of you

心存感激

Thanksgiving in heart

一路走来

All the way walking along

温暖融化

Melted by warmness

我听见冰释的声音

I heard the sound of ice melting

涓滴成溪

Dropping drops into creek

从北极奔向赤道

Running from the arctic to the equatorial

一路风浪

With waves all along the way

也有礁石

There were rocks

唯有信念

But holds the faith

支撑着溪流成河

Supporting the creek broader itself as a river, and

入海汇洋

River becomes an ocean

感恩亲情

Thanksgiving to family affection

血脉相连的关怀

Caring generated from blood connection

感恩友情

Thanksgiving to friendship

知心会意的支持

Supporing from intimate knowing

感恩爱情

Thanksgiving to Love

可遇不可求的懂得

Can be an encounter but cannot beg to meet

感恩陪伴一路走过的你们

Thanksgiving to all of you who accompanied me all the way here

萍水相逢的温暖

Phillia comes from meet by chance

感恩主

Thanksgiving to Jesus

赐予万物生长的阳光

Sunlight gave to needs of growth

平静内心的狂澜

Deep heart waves were calmed down

《塞壬之歌》[3]
SONG OF SIRENS

那不勒斯的海水

Seawater of Naples

深邃而忧伤

Deep and blue

那是因为

That is because of

阿克罗伊德斯

Akroyds

塞壬的歌声

Singing of Sirens

穿透大海穿透心脏

Penetrates the sea, penetrates the heart

　"我的睿智如普照天下的日月，

My wisdom is moon and sun, Spreading lights to the earth

深知人间发生的战争与爱情..."

Knowing deeply, war and love happened in this world"

无人可以抵挡如此的天籁

No one can resist such a tenor

甘愿为那谜厉的声音

For that blurred song

葬身不归的情海

Willing to be buried underneath of the non-return love sea

唯有英雄的奥德修斯

Hero Odysseus, is the only one

诱惑难敌的时候

When temptation unable to resist

钢索加身

He bonded himself with steel cables

用骄傲捆绑沦陷

And bundled fallen with pride

束缚了暧昧与狂乱

He restricted the ambiguous and frenzy

钢索与歌声的缠绕

The entanglement of steel cables and songs

让塞壬甘愿臣服

Make Sirens willing to subdue

葬身大海的是任性

The sea buried the capricious

升华出的永恒

Eternal sublimated from the sea

在罗马帝国的那不勒斯

In Naples of the Roman Empire

开出血色浪漫

Blood romantic blossomed

《外套》
COAT

收音机里传来辛晓琪的《味道》

"Flavor"--the song singed by Winnie Hsin comes out of radio

我披着你的外套坐在夏日的风里

I am sitting in the summer breeze with your coat on my shoulder

天上的星星闪闪烁烁

Stars blink on the sky

桌上的烛光明明暗暗

Candles blink on the table

拉紧外套我将自己裹进温暖

Pull the coat tightly, I am throwing myself into the warm

心情也突然地忽明忽暗

Mood is flickering suddenly

明朗着这份温暖的侵袭

Bright for the penetrated warmness

黯淡着自己的无助沉溺

Black for the hopeless fallen of myself

逃不脱想要逃脱的现实

Unable to escape from the reality, which I want to escape

也放不开应该放开的自作多情

Neither, unable to let the self-made passionate go, which I should let it go

多年行走在沙漠里的人

A person walking in the desert for so many years

对绿洲的渴望近乎执着到变态

Desires for oasis is almost persistent to perverted

我不知道我是爱丨温暖的感觉

I don't know if I fell in love with the warmness

还是爱上给予温暖的人

Or I fell in love with the person, who gives the warmness

只想就这样沉沦

Fallen is the only thing that I want to have now

无声无息地收藏心痛

Collecting the pain of heart silently

沉沦在时间一分一秒的流逝中

I fell down in the time pass minutes by minutes seconds by seconds

沉沦在现实虚幻的交错中

I fell into the exchanging of illusory and reality

沉沦在辛晓琪的《味道》里

I fell into the "Flavor" singed by Winne Hsin

沉沦在看着灯光下的背影

Fell into the feeling of dazing silently

默默发呆的感觉里

Watching your shadow under road lights

《水晶鞋》
A CRYSTAL SHOE

12点的钟声敲响

When o' clock hits the twelve

南瓜马车不见了

Pumpkin carriage disappears

只有灰姑娘的水晶鞋

Only a crystal shoe of Cinderella

遗落在王了的舞厅里

Left in the dancing hall of the prince

匆忙逃走的是尊严

Hurry escaped is the dignity

唯有等待一个平凡的日子

Only to wait for an ordinary day

重新穿上

Put it on again

不差分毫

Not short the least bit

即使不在辉煌的炫目中

Even it wasn' t in brilliant dazzling

平凡的光阴里

But in such an ordinary time

属于你的自然会来

If it belongs to you，it will come naturally

《花禅》
FLOWER ZEN

一花一世界

A flower /A world

一叶一菩提

A leave/A Bodhi

叶衬花馥郁

Leaves set off flowers

花红绿叶间

Flowers flash red among leaves

佛说

Buda Says

千年换得今生一回眸

Thousand years exchangs looking back in this life

花叶共相生

Flowers and Leaves living hormonally together

一花一叶一缘

A flower / A Leave / A fate

一泥一生一世

Earth/ Life/ World

Photo by: Zhao Crowley　　　　摄影：向昭

《心河》
RIVERE OF HEART

心是那

Heart is

春日暖风里的一条河

A River wondering in a warm spring day breeze

欢快地奔涌前去

Pushing ahead with joy

还是那

Or heart is

河里的藤草

A block of cane grass

缠缠绕绕

Wrap winding around

攀结着无端的心事

Unwarranted mind climbing around

心有过

It was in the heart that

恬恬淡淡的喜悦

Filled with faint joy

闪闪跳跃一河的碎金

Sparking the river with gold stars

也曾经汹汹涌涌的翻腾

It has been ranging tempestuously

彷徨无奈一河的暗流

Imitated the river with helpless undercurrent

心似那

Heart is

冬日晨阳里的河

A river in a winter morning sunlight

曾经静静地流淌

Flowing ahead silently

也曾经暗暗地忧伤

It has been secretly blue

为那有过雀跃的河谷

For the valley which ever had caper

也执着

It has been persistent

想去寻找丢失的梦想

Wish to find lost dreams

既然做河

Since being a river

就流向前方

Then flow to the front

百川归海

After all, water belongs to sea

润泽干涸的狭谷

Misting dried valley

奔向如歌的洋

Running toward sea song

生活就是这样

Life exactly like this

做出选择

How to make its choice

《雨季不再来》
NO LONGER COMES, THE RAINY SEASON

天是透明的

Sky is transparent

心，无所忧伤

Heart, has no blue

穿越往事如烟

Looking back past, the past is like mist

云淡风清

Cloud is light / breeze is soft

雨季不再来

No longer comes, the rainy season

年少的轻狂

Frivolous of youth

涩涩的懵懂

Falling in the first obscure love

随云放飞

Capricious with mood

爱情走失的那个夏日

On a summer day, love is lost

暴雨如注

In the heavily pouring

你落寞的背影

Your back appears so lonely

带着我们曾经的誓言

Took away all our oath

如流沙划过的痛，

Penetrating painful likes scratch of sands

一粒粒的真实

Each granule is a truth

也一粒粒地握不住

But neither you can hold even a single

青春的日子

In these youth days

一个人的漂泊

Drifting alone

北岸秋雨

Autumn of the Northern hemisphere

南岸春光

Spring overs the Southern

孤单的旅程何需喝彩

No need applause for the single journey

执着地前行

Keep on going persistently

只为了追逐亦不清晰的梦想

Only wish to pursue a vague dream

过往的跋涉

The previous trek

曾经的泥泞

And the ever muddy on the road

阴霾的天空

The haze sky

潮湿过的心情

And the ever wet mood

一点点的尘封

Sealed a bit by bit

虽也艰难却等得

Although it was hard, after all wait until no more,

雨季不再来

No longer comes, the rainy season

云淡风清

Clear cloud and breeze

穿越往事如烟

Looking back past, the past likes disappeared mist

心，已无所忧伤

Heart, no longer has blue

天是透明的

Sky is transparent

Photo by: Lydia Dai　摄影：戴璐

Model: Zhao Crowley　人物：向昭

《红茶咖啡》

THE MISSING PIECE

午夜电话响起

"Ring" a phone call knocks the midnight

远远近近听到那首老歌

Near and far I heard that old song

再来红茶咖啡

Came to a Café "The Missing Piece"

曾经 起喝过咖啡的地方

Where we have been for coffee

苦苦的味道

Biter flavor of coffee

不如红茶的暖

Unlike the warm taste of red tea

弥漫在心底的记忆

Memories filled the bottom of heart

好象半个世纪之久

It like that I waited for over half century long

清晰却也模糊

Clear but also vague

什么时候开始

When this begins that

学会了隐藏

I learnt hiding

以表面的无所谓

Mask face with "Does Not A Matter"

执拗着心底的自尊

I persist hold on self-esteem from the bottom of heart

放任一把火焰

Let it be, the fire

独自燃烧

Burning by itself

燃在岁月的炼炉里

Burning in the fireplace of time

慢慢煨成一杯红茶

Slowly, brewing a cup of red tea

啜饮点滴的涩

Taste the astringent a bit by bit

失落在The Missing Piece

I lost in The Missing Piece

Photo by: Zhao Crowley　　　摄影：向昭

《等待》
WAIT

一卷诗书

A poetry book

油墨泫然

Inky all over

多少的等待

How many waits

黯然的夜色

Until dark nights fallen

电台依旧

The radio station is still the same

只是茫然了频道

Only the channel was changed

等一份懂得

Wait for a comprehend

化尽冰霜

To burn all the ice and frost

用火焰的热度

With fire temperature

温暖内心的苍凉

To warm the coldness inside of the heart

《圣诗教堂》
HILLSONG CHURCH

"如果你相信生命永恒

If you believe in eternal life

请你也相信上帝

Please be faithful to God

上帝将爱恩赐

Because the LOVE God give to us

更改我们的生命

Will transfer our life

我们将在天堂相遇

In the heaven, you will be found

坐在Hillsong的教堂

Sit in the Hillsong Church

聆听福音

Listen to the Gospel

泪流满面

Tears run down along my face

是因为心灵的触动

It was the soul that is touched

过往的一年

In the past whole year

行走在起伏跌宕的山巅谷底

Walking along the summits and valleys, up and down

在心上雕刻

Carving on the heart

疼痛与快乐

Pains and joys

也想用心

Wish to carve by heart

雕一幅经典

And carve a master piece

表达从不曾有过的体会

To express the experience never had before

但初学的手多么笨拙

But hands are so awkward because of a beginning learner

涂涂抹抹

Applied and smeared

聚合分离

Polymerization separation

人间常态

It was normal in the world of human being

重新握住上帝的手

Grab hands of God again

新的一年

In this coming new year

祈祷灵魂的重铸

Pray for a new created soul

在心上慢慢雕刻

Carving on the heart slowly and slowly

属灵的契合

To fit in the belong spirit

《爱情刻刀》
LOVE BURIN

爱情是一把刻刀

Love is a burin

随岁月留痕

Time passing by, carving left marks

循心而刻

Carving alongside heart

雕刻欢乐

Carving joyful

雕刻甜蜜

Carving sweetness, and

也雕刻疼痛

Carving painful

与悲伤

Carving sadness

如果不爱

If there is no love

请不要轻易拿起这把刻刀

Please don't take up this burin

无爱的手雕刻不出经典

A masterpiece cannot be carved without love

等到听说爱情回来过

Until it was said that love has once returned back

已千帆过尽空留心河枯竭

Thousands of sails passed and left drought in the heart river

如若有爱

If love is there

也请尽心雕刻

Please be careful of using this burin

偏走的刀锋

The blade off burin

只会血刃

Only would be a blood blade

等到听说爱情回来过

Until it was said that love has once returned back

也只徒留想见不敢见的伤痛

Only the painful from the longing to see but dare not to meet burnt

《一路平安》
BE SAFE ON THE WAY

今晚的月光清辉满地

Moonlight tonight fills clear on the earth

我想起将要走在路上的朋友

I remember my friend who is going to take off home

一程又一程

A journey after another

我们来来回回

We come and go

带着过客的角色

Play the role of a passing by guest

于这世间行

Walking in this world

或许是为了追寻梦想

May be for pursuing a dream

亦或许只是为了看一道道风景

Or may be only wish to see views on the road

远处的山丘延绵起伏

Rolling hills in distance

我们的眼望不到尽头

Eyesight can not reach the unlimited end

迷惘着幻想风光旖旎

Feel lost but still imagine beautiful sceneries

却忘了备足行囊

Yet forget to prepare sufficient luggage

忘了道路会泥泞

Forget the possible muddy of the road

需要备一颗跨越阻碍的心

Need a prepared heart to cross over blocks

一路前行

All the way ahead

有朋友相伴是福分

It is a blessing to have friends accompanied

但孤单也会一程程

But the loneliness could be with you, a journey after a journey

艰难只能自己扛

Obstructs only can be faced by yourself

扛过了千山万水

After crossing over thousands of miles

找到属于自己的风景

Until you find views belongs to your own

相信终有一道彩虹是为自己绚烂

Believe, there would be a rainbow shinning out only for yourself

彼时此刻的行里

In that and this time itinerary

唯祝你顺其自然

Only wish you "Let it be"

一路平安

Be safe on the way

《城里的月光》
MOONLIGHT OF THE CITY

小时候住过的城

The city I lived in my childhood

是一座古城

Is a city with long history

绕城的墙四四方方的敦厚

The surrounding city wall is square and thick

夜晚护城河水里有清亮的月光

There were clear moonlights spread in the moat circles the wall, and

城根有煽着蒲扇的姥姥讲故事

My grandma sits at the root of the city wall telling stories

心境纯纯地透亮

Hearts of kids are pure and clear

月光圆过又缺过

Moon sometimes is round and sometimes is slim

聚聚散散地就离了老城来新城

Union, separate, left the old city and came to a new city

新城在地球的南端

The new city locates in the southern hemisphere

却没有古老的四方的墙

Yet there is no square and thick city wall

新城的月光依样清亮

Moonlight of the new city is also clear

印在情人港的海湾里

Spreading lights in the bay of Darling Harbour

讲故事的姥姥已在天堂

Grandma has gone to the heaven

想起那些听过的故事

Those stories still live in my memory

编成诗歌几行

Compose them in poem collection

找回一段心境纯纯的时光

Memory the time when had pure and clear heart

听说故乡的墙依然四方

I heard that the city wall of hometown is still square and thick

只是有霾雾重重

However the blue sky is covered by smog

护城的水中是否还印着清亮的月光

Is there still clear moonlight spread in the city moat

记取着千年的传说

Records the legend of thousands years

晨钟暮鼓的时光

Morning bells and night drums

在那古城穿梭

Shuttle through that old city

何时驱散锁雾重重

When smog can be dispersed

重见天光

Returns the blue sky

换回古朴的心境纯纯

Returns the simple pure and clear heart

《想和你再去吹吹风》
WISH TO HAVE A JOYRIDE WITH YOU AGAIN

坐在闺蜜的红色敞篷里

Sitting in my girlfriend's red convertible car

滚石的音乐震耳欲聋

The rocks heavy metal music is so loud to deafening

带着友情

Take our friendship

我们一起去海边吹吹风

Let's go for a joyride

想起我们十七年的情谊

Our friendship has been for over 17 years

从一无所有

Started from when we had nothing, and

忧心未来在异国漂泊

Worried the drifting future in this foreign country

到锦袍加身

Until now we have silk cloth jade food, and

香车驰骋在他乡旅途

This luxury car gallop on the foreign land

我们也曾是柔弱女子

We had been soft weak girls

如今练成傲骨侠身的女汉子

However, today we are strong female with self-pride bones and

chivalrous body

闺蜜们携手走来

Hand in hand, Ladies friendship

一起笑过，一起哭过

We laughed, we cried

一起闹过，一起拥抱过

We were troubled, we were hold on each other

生活的酸甜苦辣

Five-spice flavor of the life

情感的高低起伏

Ups and downs of our emotions

与你们一同分享

We have shared together

没有秘密的情谊细水长流

The friendship without secret keeps longer

听你娓娓讲述成长的痛与悟

I listen to your story about pain and awaken in growth

陪我一起安抚内心的伤与憾

You accompany and comfort me when I am sad and blue

我们一起感动

We are touched

相约一起快乐着老去

We agreed getting old slowly in joy

闺蜜是一生的投资

Ladies' friendship is a life investment

回收的是满心的温暖

Return is the warm of the whole heart

有你们

Having you all

真的很好

Is really good

Photo by: Lydia Dai　摄影：戴璐

《路遇的烟花》
ROADSIDE FIREWORK

路遇的烟花

Encountered incidentally, roadside firework

在悉尼港的上空绽放

Blooming over in the sky above the Sydney Harbor

姹紫嫣红的火焰

Brilliant colors of flame

腾空又落入海水

Vacated up then felt into bay water

与星辉映

Shining with stars

与水交融

Blended with water

悉尼桥上碌碌的车流

Busy car flows on the Sydney Bridge

匆忙着

Hurrying through

行人却闲散着漫步

Pedestrians walk on their own leisure pace

我与闺蜜

I with my girlfriend

挽着臂膀

Hold on hands

看这偶遇的美丽

Watching this beautiful scene

聊一路的过往未来

Walking on the bridge and chatting about the future

回味着一起美食的快乐

Recalling garments we enjoyed just then

简简单单的时光在友情中穿过

The friendship cross over between us in this simple time

我说，或许十年后的某天

I said, maybe one day in a decade later

我会再次想起今晚的烟花

I would remember the flame of tonight

那时的想起

When remembered at that time

或许我会庆祝生命的绽放与灿烂

I may be being celebrate the bloom and brilliant of my life

也或许我会遗憾

Or I may feel pity

囿于踯躅

I was prisoned into today's silly ambulate

我会错过一些本该的美好

I would miss some glorious supposed to be in the life

当人生走在十字路口

When life facing the cross

你是否会选择那条有烟花在前的路

Would you choose the one ahead with the brilliant firework

《默》
SILENT

蝴蝶有翅膀

Butterflies have wings

在天上飞

Flying on sky

兔子有腿

Rabbits have legs

在草里蹦跳

Jumping in grass

鱼儿划水在海里游

Fish swims in sea

而我是一条美人鱼

And I am a mermaid

剪开鱼尾当双脚的美人鱼

A mermaid with feet, which was cut from my fish tail

本该沉没在海底的王宫

I suppose to stay in the King Palace at the deep bottom of the sea

看珊瑚变幻的色彩

Watching the changing colors of corals

听海马的呢喃细语

Listening to the whispers of sea horse

但我只是看了波光粼粼的海面一次

But I raised up my head and watched out the shimmering sea surface

就望见了你

I saw you

望见了你不可抵挡的阳光面容

Saw your sunny face, which is irresistible

心中驻进了彩虹

A rainbow rooted into my heart

用每一脚的疼痛试图靠近

I am trying to step closer to you with painful on each step

然而风浪那么大

However, the waves are so huge

鱼尾变成的双脚无法坚强

The feet come from the fish tail is not strong enough

随波逐流

Drifting with waves

变成白浪的泡沫

Became as white foams

失去我的灵魂

Lost my soul

海巫早已预言了这个童话的结局

The sea wizard predicted such ending of this fairy tale

但我想

But I knew

没有灵魂的泡沫不该有痛吧

The foams without soul should not have pains

Photo by: Selina Luo　摄影：罗景泊

Model: Zhao Crowley　人物：向昭

《颠沛流离》
VAGRANT LIFE

一路走过

All the way come

颠沛流离

Led a vagrant life

愿有人陪你

Wish you are accompanied

看遍繁华

Experienced all the prosperous

也历尽风霜

And crossed over all difficulties

别说辛苦

Never said hard

风光都在顶峰处

Good views are all located on the summit

云遮雾障

Clouds covered and fog blocked

唯有太阳的光辉

Only when sunlights

突破洒落

Breaks through and spreads

春风秋雨如沐

Bath in Spring breeze and Autumn rains

回首笑面风云

Looking back and laughing that storming time

愿有人陪你

Wish you were accompanied

颠沛流离

Went through the vagrant life

如果没有

If weren not

愿你成为自己的太阳

Wish you became a sun of yourself

《沉默就是一首诗》
SILENT IS A POEM

沉默就是一首诗

Silent is a poem

我的心有点累

My heart feels a bit tired

却又在暗夜的时光里无法入睡

But I cannot fell into sleep in this dark night

夜的苍穹

Sky of night

繁星点点

Decorated by stars

我却找不到那一丝光明

Yet I cannot find even a bit bright

只有沉默

Only silent

可以与黑暗抗衡

Counterbalances the darkness

假装一片和谐的色调

Pretend to be a harmony

沉默也是一种慢性病

Silent is a chronic illness

找不到医治的良方

Unable to find a curable meditation

只有在暗夜的吞噬中

Only hides inside of the night swallow

一步步地沉沦

Degradation steps by steps

慢慢地打开伤口

Torn the wound to open slowly

又一点点的封锁

And seals it again a bit by bit

直到走出那片霾雾

Until walk out of that smog

直到等来救赎的阳光

Until wait and gain that salvation sunlight

再也感觉不出疼痛

Until no longer feel pains

《爱而不得》

LOVE BUT UNABLE TO GET

佛说：得即失，失即得

Buddha says: gain is loss, loss is gain

爱情里最美丽的一种

The most beautiful kind in love

就是爱而不得

Is that "Love, but unable to get"

世俗的世界里

In this ordinary world

太多的条件

Too much conditions

凡夫俗子的我们不得不苟且的存在

Ordinary people like us has no choice but must be alive perfunctorily

心中有诗和远方

Poem and distance exist in heart

理想的家园只在梦中

The ideal homeland exists in dreams

为了活着

In order to make a living

我们打拼

We fight

不断的屈服于现实的压迫

Give up to pressures of reality

但我知道

But I knew

心灵的深处

Deep in heart

有那么一方净土

There is a clean place

为爱情保留

Was kept only for love

用柏拉图的精神

Platonic spirit

让失即得的永存

Make the "loss is gain" lasting forever

始终欠下一句感谢

From the start to the end, "Thanks" is owed

这一世的美丽

The beauty of this life, is a

就是永远的朋友

Forever friend

《好久不见》
LONG TIME NO SEE

来到这个老地方

Come to this old place

我在午夜的钟声里

In the sound of midnight bell

独自徘徊

I am wondering around

街角的灯光隐隐烁烁

Lights at the street corner faint and flickering

咖啡店里早已昏暗

Inside café became dark

晚餐后的咖啡一杯一杯喝不断

I drink after dinner coffees cups by cups

谁来陪伴

Who will come to accompany

零点午夜后的不眠

The sleepless night after the midnight

只为等你

I am here only to wait for you

接连不断的坏消息

Heard so many consistent bad news recently

渐悟人生无常

I was enlightenment the impermanent of life

存在与失去只在天地转换一瞬间

It is just a second between the exchanges of exist and extinct

荣华富贵又如何

What a matter, rich or prospers

一口白粥青菜的家常

Plain porridge and ordinary vegetables in family daily life

有温情相伴

With warm accompany

才能不枉曾为世间客

Then you could say you were a guest of this life

可遇不可求的缘

Fate, which can be met but cannot beg

修炼轮回几生

Practice, reincarnation for several lifetimes

才敢如此念念不忘

Dare not forget like this

朋友，别来无恙

My friend, hope that you were well

好久不见

No see for such a long time

《如何》
HOW

如何

How

才能走出心的围城

Come out of the sealed city of heart

看天上

Look upon the sky

云卷云舒

Cloud close, cloud spread

自由地变换飞扬

Change, flying freely

如何

How

才能淡出花开的芬芳

Fade out of the fragrance of flowers

看水中

Look down the water

浮萍落叶

Duckweed and fallen leaves

寂寂满池繁华旖旎

Loneliness filled the pond full with crowded waves

如何

How

缘尽才能散去不惮忧伤

Fate scattered and separated without fear of sadness

听雨落

Listen to the rhythm sound of falling rains

打湿初见的微笑

Wetted the smiles, which was the one when we first met

朦胧了双眸

Eyes blurred

诉不尽别离的感伤

Without ending saying the sentimentality of leave

如何

How

才能学会坚硬起心怀

To learn harden the heart

选择理想之路

Choose the ideal avenue

扫尽满目的风霜

Swapping away all the frost ahead

即使前途迷惘

Even there is perplex in the front

也能不屈我愿

Cannot give up my will

重归苏莲托的梦乡

Return to the dreamed Sorrento

《晚安》
GOOD NIGHT

睡吧睡吧

Sleep, sleep

象个孩子一样

Like a child

在夏夜的南风里

In the southern breeze of this summer night

忘记一切的烦恼和忧伤

Let's forget all the worries and blue

让我们回到最初的状态

Let's back to the initial status

心无杂念地相望而笑

Look at each other and smile with peace in the heart

人生只如初见

If the life likes the first time meet

那一刻的美好

The beautiful of that moment

已沁入整个心田

Rooted in the whole heart

曾经的桩桩件件

The scenes ever happened

记忆满怀

Recorded in a whole heart

心存感激

Thanksgivings inside

也带上勇气

Take your courage

一往而前

Keep on going

一切顺由天意

Follow God's will

稳稳的安心

Peace in mind

无悔就好

All good without regret

晚安好梦

Good dream, good night

《活在当下》
LIVE AT THE MOMENT

清风问白云

Soft breeze asks white cloud

你为什么飘在蓝色的天空

Why are you flying over the blue-sky

白云悠闲地赶路没有回答

Cloud is leisurely keeping on going and didn't answer

绿叶问清风

Green leave asks soft breeze

你的轻拂为什么会让我沙沙地歌唱

Why your soft touch could make me singing Shalala

清风淡淡地拂过却没有回答

Soft breeze touched it softly but didn't answer

猫儿问绿叶

A cat asks green leaves

你为什么经历了秋雨就会飘落枯寂

Why are you fallen and dried after experienced the autumn rain

绿叶轻叹生命的无常没有回答

Green leaves sighed on impermanence life but didn't answer

大地问猫儿

Land asks cat

你问什么紧靠大地才会如此闲适快乐

Why are you always so happy when you roll over the land

猫儿回答说

Cat answers

我没有翅膀就不会象白云一样漂浮

I have no wings and cannot fly like white clouds

我留恋我领地就不会象清风一样无踪

I love my territory and won't leave my land like soft breeze

身靠土地就不会如绿叶一般绚丽一时

When I am down to the earth, I won't like green leaves just be brilliant

for a moment

活在当下

I live at the moment

我无忧无虑

I have no worries

明天太阳升起

When sun rises up again tomorrow

为梦想逡巡过

I patrolled for my dreams

我就是快乐的喵星人

I am a happy cat in the cat star

Photo by: Zhao Crowley   摄影：向昭

《悄》
QUIET

夜色寂寂

Loneliness night

陪你在黑暗里

I am with you sitting in the dark

风无语

Wind keeps quiet

星无语

Star keeps quiet

月无语

Moon keeps quiet

小虫儿偶鸣

Occasionally little crickets singing

心无语

Heart keeps quiet

一路的走来

All the way here

多少风霜

How much frost

多少次的踢不烂

How much fought for lasting forever

看日升月落的悄悄

Sun rises and moon sinks quietly

听心的慢悟

Listen to the slow words of heart

默契的懂得已入骨

Tacit understanding is already carved deeply in bones

何以铭心

What is to carve in heart

泪无语

Tears keep quiet

《南半球的夏天》
THE SUMMER OF THE SOUTHERN HEMISPHERE

南半球的夏天

The summer of the Southern Hemisphere

二月的风

Wind of February

带着火热的翅膀

With the wings of fire

扫遍每一个角落

Swapping each corner

这是季节的风

This is the seasonal wind

带着欢悦的响铃

Brings the joyful bell with it

驯鹿的脚趾没有雪迹

The reindeer's foot has no trace of snow

它们送来热气腾腾的夏日

They take a hot summer day here

哈利路亚

Hallelujah

消除你的忧伤

The wind swapped away of your blue

南半球的二月里

In February of the southern hemisphere

用火热备份所有的岁月

Backup all the days with your enthusiasm

无论你要去往哪里

Wherever you go

不要让心再次冰冻

Don't let the heart frozen again

《乡愁》
HOMESICK

乡愁

Homesick

是一碗扯面

Is a bowl of hand made noodle

一端牵着古城长安

One side holds the old city Chang' An

　端牵着新城悉尼

One side links the new city Sydney

漫漫蜿蜒的滋味是酸辣

Meander along with the flavor of sour and spicy

酸酸的是背井离乡

The sour flavor comes from quit away of hometown

辣辣的是儿女情长

The spicy flavor is from the girl of hometown I miss

乡愁

Homesick

是一份肉夹馍

Is a hometown hanburger

心里夹着浓浓的香醇

Inside is the thick mellow

外面背着厚厚的面壳

Wrapped the outside with a thick bread

长长久久的味道是追忆

The long lasting flavor is my memory

追那似水年华的青春

To memory lost youth in the past

忆那岁月流殇的感叹

To memory the flying of time

乡愁

Homesick

是年端的一份思念

Is a miss hit on at this end of the year

思一声乡音的撩拨

Miss the tease dial of the dialect

念一句秦腔的韵吼

Miss the charm roar opera from Qin

惆惆怅怅的是丽人佳影

Melancholy of the pretty girl of hometown

远方诗依然

I am writing a poem in the remote new city

倩影何在兮

But, where is the beauty of my hometown

Photo by: Zhao Crowley　　　摄影：向昭

《愿温暖同行》
WISH JOURNEY ACAMPNIED BY WARMTH

爱过的心如何变淡

How to shade out a heart, which felt in love before

看这世界纷纷扰扰

Watching the disturbance of the world

有多少真心只为爱而追逐

How many true hearts exist merely for pursuing love

不过是繁华名利但为己心

Most are just for pursuing wealth to own heart benefit

爱过的心如何变淡

How to shade out a heart, which felt in love before

可以甘愿拱手托付

Wish to entrust love per your will

却戚戚何人可与风雨相依

Yet worries, who would be the one shares wind and storm

一粥一饭一茶一饮

A bowl of porridge, a cup of tea

平平淡淡唯是真

The more plainer the more true

爱过的心如何变淡

How to shade out a heart, which felt in love before

放任相逐翱翔自由

Let it fly to chase, to be free

唯愿天宽海阔

Wish sky broad enough and sea much wider

有温暖关怀同舟共济

With warm care，support and help on the same boat

奔生命之理想

Pursue dreamed life

笑看风云叱姹时

Laughing and saw situation coveted

《爱的空气》
LOVE IS IN THE AIR

Love is in the air

空气中爱情在流动

I'm at my girlfriend's wedding

我在闺蜜的婚礼上

Feel the atmosphere of love

感受这爱的气氛

Something touched the depth of my heart

灵魂的深处被触动

I must meet you from my last life

我们一定相遇在前世

And we promised that we would find each other in this life

约定了来到今生彼此相寻

When we met, tears in eyes, pains in heart

当我们相逢，泪眼婆娑，痛在心里

We recognized each other at the first glance

我们一眼就能彼此相认

Although the soup of PoPo Meng[4] made us lost the memory

虽然孟婆汤让我们失去了记忆

The feelings of love would never disappear

爱的感觉却从未消失

Almost forgot what the kiss taste like

几乎忘记了亲吻的滋味

It happened only in my dream

那些只在梦里回还

How could I break the lock of my heart

我要如何冲破心的枷锁

Throw myself into the air of love

将自己扔进爱情的空气中

Just like I am in the dream

一如自己在梦中

Without fear and block

一如自己在梦中无所畏惧与禁锢

I'm just myself follow my heart

我只是跟从己心

Follow the love in the air

跟随爱情的空气

I'm just myself wanting to see you again in the reincarnation

我只是跟随自己，想要再次的轮回相遇

Photo by: Zhao Crowley   摄影：向昭

《随缘》

UP TO FATE

自从奥林匹斯山上的神

Since the God in the Olympia mountain

一把斧子劈开

Split human into half with an ax

苍穹之下就有了寻觅

Searching the other half comes into being

一半是海水

One half is like sea water

一半是火焰

The other half is like fire

遇上便是一场短兵相接的圆满

Once encountered, it would be a reunion through a battle

看不见的磁场

Invisible magnetic field

看得见的相随

Visible follow up

纷纷绕绕

One after another round

锁雾重重

Heavy fog layers after layers

130

刀光剑影

Sword lights and sword shadow

原以为

Initially thought

可以善托

Able to hand over with care

却未知生命不能承受之轻

Yet, unable to know that life is not able to bear the lightness

我是谁

Who I am

他是谁

Who he is

你又是谁

And who you are

不为一刀的分体

If not the half from the same split

何来道同的默契

Where comes the tacit agreement

罢了

Let it pass

随缘进退

Forward and back with fate

唯顺己心

Follow your heart

《无围之城》
UNSEALED CITY

筑一座无围之城

Built an unsealed city

用缘锁定

Lock it by fate

心门无界

No boundary to heart door

诚意为疆

Sincerity is the territory

品城内花开花谢

Appreciate flowers bloom and flowers fell inside the city

渡城外冬去春来

Ford the winters gone and springs come outside the city

小桥流水

Petty bridge flowing water

夕阳余晖

Sunset left afterglow

你不经意地来来去去

Yours come and go inadvertently

碰触了无端的谁的心事

Whose unconscious mind was touched

俯首闲捡枝叶

Bowing down to pick up leaves and branches casually

抬头遍数浮云

Look up to count over the flirting cloud

化心为简

Turn heart into simple

无念无求

Without expecting and begging

随遇而安

Take things as they come

《十面埋伏》
AMBUSH ALL AROUND

仿佛一场战斗

As if in a battle

我陷在十面埋伏里

I was tracked in the ambush all around

我在人群中尽力地突围

I tried my best to break through the crowd

却也走不出你编织的网

Yet, I cannot break through the web you weaved

善意的围困

Sieged by good wills

无声的劝谏

Advise in silence

让我思悟直面人生的谜境

Make me think and face to the enigma life

一道道的考题累积

Accumulated questions

梦回那年的黑色七月[5]

Take me back to the black July of that year

我埋头在无尽的题库中

Buried myself in the countless questions

奋笔疾书自己也不清楚的答案

Writing down answers I am even not sure of

谁来营救

Who comes to save

骑上一匹白马

Riding on a white horse

战袍横刀

With combat robe and battle sword

为胜局加冕之时

When time comes to crown the winning

尊为王者

He would be named as king

《最后的夏日》
LAST DAY OF THE SUMMER

Whispering, the wind of south

南风轻轻吹过

Summer of the Southern Hemisphere

南半球的夏天

Reached its last day

来到了最后一日

All the agitated passion

那些曾经激荡过的热情

Gradually, gradually, cooling down

渐渐地平息

Sink in the sea of memories

沉淀在记忆的海洋里

Two lines steps are still lying on the beach

沙滩上的脚印依旧两行

Where have the chasing couples gone

追逐的人儿却无踪影

Blueness of autumn comes close slowly

秋天的忧伤慢慢靠近

The about leaving season

就要离开的季节

Shaking the died leaves off to fill the yard

摇落满院的枯叶

Little cat chasing mice and playing

逐鼠而戏的小猫

Eyes filled in by silly and bud

目光蠢萌

He rubs my ankle with cuties

蹭着我的腿腕而娇

How could I not

怎么舍得

Hold you into my hug

不拥你入怀

Gone after all, the summer

夏天，终究的逝去

The coming autumn, would you also bring full colors

秋天，会否依然色彩斑斓

In the days of drifting

漂泊依旧的时日

Where is the home of my heart

心归何

Photo by: Zhao Crowley　　　摄影：向昭

《虚拟世界》
INTERNET WORLD

现实里有一个世界

In the real world

我们相遇

We met

第一眼的看见

At the first glance

我却把你错放进了虚拟的世界

I dragged you into the Internet world by mistakc

那里的我们戏闹追逐

There, we follow each other and play

不经意就点燃了一把火焰

Accidently, we started a fire

一次回眸

Looked back once

虚拟的光环照亮的面庞

There was a face light up by aura, and

让我不由自主地想靠近

Attracted my helpless approaching

想和你笑

Wish to laugh with you

想和你闹

Wish to fight with you

也不介意你看见我流淌的眼泪

Neither mind seeing my tears by you

现实世界里难以实现的天荒地老

Unable to realize the long lasting and keeping forever in the reality

放在虚拟的世界里地久天长

Leave it to be eternal in the internet world

风雨也不湿的脚步

Steps cannot be wet by wind and rain

只为追赶晴时的彩虹

Merely for pursing rainbow in the fine weather day

或许要跨过鸿沟

May need to cross over impassable chasm

或许也要历尽磨难

May have to go through all the turbulences

既然选择了前方

Since chose the front

我就不会退缩

I would not withdraw

《放晴》
COME SHINE

看一片蓝天

Watching a block of blue sky

让心情慢慢放晴

Let heart come shine

这个城市

This city

离海那么近

Is so close to sea

用一份初心耕耘

Cultivating and weeding with an initial heart

种一海的勿忘我

Grow a seabed Forget-Me-Not

春暖时节

When spring comes

花开浅蓝

Blooming light blue all over the sea

种满心的红玫瑰

Planting a heart-bed red rose

面海慰心

Comforting heart when face the sea

馥郁芬芳

Fragrant sweet smelling

两个季节的漫长

Cross two seasons' long

秋雨冬寒

Autumn rain and winter coldness

过后的春天就不会太远

Afterwards, it would not be too far to meet spring

《习惯》
HABIT

习惯了在清晨的时光里

It's a habit that in morning

喝一杯苦咖

Drink a cup of biter coffee

强行赶去熬夜的疲惫

Force away fatigue from a sleepless night

习惯了在午后的阳光下

It's a habit that under sunlight of an afternoon

寻找温暖

Searching for warmth

融化一点内心深处的冰寒

To melt icy cold comes from depth of heart

习惯了接近零点的午夜

It is a habit that at 12 o' clock midnight

写一首小诗

Write a poem

把零零落落的心情揉进笔墨

Rub the bits here and there mood into a pen

习惯了为诗配一支歌

It's a habit that choose a song to match the poem

想象自己是童话城堡里的公主

Imagine that I was a princess living in a fairy tale castle

等待无惧的他成就不一样的救赎

Waiting for an unfear him come to save

习惯了的习惯

It's a habit that to be accustomed to

塑造了我的两面

Build two faces of me

在网络间高调地行走

Walking in the Internet world in high tone

在现实中平庸地沉默

Keeping silence in ordinary reality

打破习惯的力量

Break through strength of the habit

重新建立自由王国

Rebuilt a free kingdom

黑羽白羽，都是天鹅

No matter with black or white feather, swans are swans

悲喜人生，冷暖自知

Sad or happy, knew by self, whether it is a cold or warm life

Photo by: Zhao Crowley　　　摄影：向昭

《极》
EXTREME

黑的反面是白

Opposite of Black is white

白的反面是红

Opposite of white is red

万物相克也相生

The universe interact with each other

唯心而论

Spiritualist says

一个事物可以有多极的解释

There are several utmost points in one fact

唯理而言

Rationalist says

同一匹马不能同时踏入两条河流

A horse cannot step in two rivers simultaneously

而两条河流可以同时汇入同一大海

But two rivers can join in one sea at the same time

今日的苦难可能是为了明日的欢颜

Today's suffer could be for the exchange of tomorrow's smiling face

所有遭遇过的都不会是白白的浪费

All encountered won't be just a waste

当我们趟过时间的漩流

When we crossed over the time whirlpool

是是非非

Right or wrong

终将是极的各端

It is just the utmost point of it

五彩缤纷只凭各心

Multicolor relays on multi hearts

《假如爱有天意》
IF THERE IS DECREE FOR LOVE

假如爱有天意

If there is decree for love

无论星移斗转

No matter how stars change their positions

顺其自然就好

It would be good to let it be

假如爱有天意

If there is decree for love

无论相聚分离

No matter union or separate

随遇而安就好

It would be good to let it be

假如爱有天意

If there is decree for love

无需刻意追逐

No need to chase up on purpose

相守相伴就好

It would be good to just hold on and accompany

150

假如爱有天意

If there is decree for love

无论地老天荒

No matter the earth getting elder and the sky became fallow

活在当下就好

It would be good to live at the moment

《铿锵玫瑰》

WILDERNESS ROSE

他们都说她是一朵铿锵玫瑰

They all said that she's a wilderness rose

无惧风雨的摧折

No fear of destroyed by storms

无畏霜雪的打压

No fear of suppressed by frost and snow

可有谁知道

However, who knows

内心的卑微

Inside of her humble

是为爱而执着

Is persistence for pursuing love

以为可以换取的深情

Suppose that waiting could exchange deep love

只不过是风中的虚幻

Yet, it was illusory that drifting in wind

盛开的玫瑰即便铿锵

Even the blooming rose is so tough

也终不能敌时光的荏苒

It can not withstand time elapse quickly

在沉默的对峙中枯萎

Withered in silent confrontation

衰退的是曾经的娇艳

Fading the tender and beautiful of the ever

落地化泥的是花瓣雨

Became petal rain when fell down to the earth

焚心以火

Burry heart with fire

葬心以冰

Burry heart with ice

笑面冷漠

Smiling face indifferent heart

直言无谓

Said, "Doesn' t Matter" directly

Photo by: Zhao Crowley 摄影：向昭

《一半、一半》
HALF, HALF

一半是乌云，一半是蓝天

Half are dark clouds, half is a blue-sky

云端中透出太阳的光芒

Sunlight penetrates through clouds

一半是海水，一半是路途

Half are seawaters, half is a journey ahead

脚下行走的是远方的理想

Steps underneath are ideals of distance

一半是绿树，一半是西风

Half are green trees, half is west wind

遥遥相望的是钢筋水泥的倒影

Watching further away is shade covered by steels and concretes

心情一半是阴霾，一半是靓丽

Half mood is haze, half moods are nice

阴霾着走不出的感伤

Haze for the blue unable to escape

靓丽着激情挑战的未来

Nice for the future assigned to challenge

把自己活成一棵树的模样

Alive yourself in a shape of tree

根在土里深埋

Rooting deeply in earth

叶在空中婆娑

Whirling leaves in the air

任狂风暴雨浇淋

Despite the pouring shower of storming

把骄傲站成风雨之后的清丽

Stand pride in beauty after rains

在暗夜里孤独

Lonely in dark nights

在阳光下灿烂

Shinning in brilliant sunlight

《窗外》
OUTSIDE THE WINDOW

秋雨，淅淅沥沥，漫洒窗外

Autumn rains, Shalala, sprinkle all over outside of window

寂静，独守一窗，与心沈淀

Silence, defend alone the window, precipitating with heart

淡然，滑动指尖，翻阅往事

Indifferently, move fingers; turn over stories of past

尘封，彼情此心，仿若眼前

Sealed, that beloved and this heart, as if still ahead of eyes

雨季里花开

Flowers bloom in the rain season

雨季里花落

Flowers fell in the rain season

默默渲染一世的盛与衰

Silently, rendering centuries ladle and feeble

曾几何时欢颜的双舞双飞

Two people's dancing and flying in smile faces of whenever

换做今宵独步的我行我素

Changed into tonight's only step of my own walking and way

痴情总被无情笑

Infatuation is always laughed by heartless

雨落葬花独黛玉[6]

Daiyu is the only girl who buried flowers felt in rains

香冢叹息梦一空

Sigh the in vain of dream at her scant tomb

利禄功名众宝钗[7]

Most people learn from Baochai and chasing rich and fame

玉食锦衣心积重

Jade food silk cloth blocked the heavy heart

也道：虚空、虚空

Sigh continues: Empty, Empty

《回到从前》
RETURN TO THE PAST

南风轻拂

Soft touch by the southern breeze

是否来自故乡的挪缕

Is this the one comes from the hometown

白云飘荡

White clouds fly above

是否同样明亮的天空

Is there the same bright sky?

软泥青草 散发着乡愁的氤氲

Slime and green grass emit the homesick air

是否还能回到从前

If return to the past can be realized

无愁的欢颜 任意书写

Smile face with no worry writes at will

不羁的故事 旖旎绚丽

Unruly stories are charming and gorgeous

一路看尽蜿蜒的风光

Zig zag views all along the way

如果可以再回到从前

If returning to the past can be achieved

我愿备份记忆的行囊

I would back up memories in the luggage

在未来的某天翻阅

Looking back on a day in the future

让所有的喜怒哀乐 抚平皱褶的心情

Let all the emotions to iron the wrinkle mood flat

即便雨季也不畏潮湿

It won't be wetted again even in a rain season

《季节》

SEASON

夏去秋来

Sumer has gone and Autumn comes

火热散尽的时候

When fervent fully disappeared

蛰伏在冬天的寒中蓄积能量

Hibernate in winter cold to accumulate energy

岁月沉淀

Time precipitin

静静地品味不同季节的美

Appreciating unique beautiful of different seasons in the silence exchange

虽然没有了轻装飘逸

Although taking off the elegant from light clothes

冬的厚重可以让你成长

The heavy of winter made growth of things

等待春天的破茧蝶出

Waiting until cocoons out of spring butterfly

化丝成翅迎着阳光飞舞

Change silk into wings dancing flying greeting sun

穿越花香

Cross over floral

频采蜜糖

Busy in collecting honeys

季节啊季节

Season / season

请你放慢脚步

Please slow down your steps

细细品味冰火冷暖

Appreciating flavors of icy, fire, cold and warm

让心

Let heart

随风轻盈

Lithesome with breeze

随霜寒冷

Frigid with frost

也随太阳热烈

Animate with sun

随风暴历练

Temper with storm

体验生活的浮浮沉沉

Experience the floating and sinking of the life

《星烛》
STAR CANDLE

雨季初晴的黄昏

Twilight of an early clear day in the rain season

微风轻轻轻轻地透过露台

Breeze softly, softly, penetrates through the terrace

吹进寥落的小屋

Penetrates through the lonely small room

抬头看天

Looking up to sky

云脚慢慢慢慢地走

Cloud walks slowly / slowly

推散几缕乌云

Scattered a few black clouds

南十字的星光隐隐隐隐地透出

The light of Southern Cross Star revealed faintly / faintly

坐在一室的暗里

Sitting in darkness at the corner of the room

不开灯

Lights were not turned on

只让星辉点点点点地洒进心里

Only allows star lights spilled into heart little bit by bit

明亮角落的潮湿

Lighting the corner feebly

不知这星光能否

Not knowing whether this bit star lights

就此住进心室

Would enter into the room of heart

如明烛点亮渐渐渐渐燃尽

Like a bright candle lighting up till the end eventually / eventually

却能样放炙热的温度

It is able to release hot temperature

恒久恒久的芬芳

Fragrance lasts forever / forever

《一些梦想》

SOME DREAMS

一个人的行走

One person's walking

在这繁华的街头

On this busy street

人潮涌动熙熙攘攘

Tides of people crowded the way

苟且的生活

Careless life

缠绕着琐碎烦恼

Enlaced the trivial worries

什么时候

When

慢慢淡忘了诗的感觉

Slowly forget the feels of poem

买一束应季的鲜花

Purchased a bunch of seasonal flower

没有诗的时候

When there is no poem

至少应该有花香

At least there should have fragrance of flowers

音乐响起

Lights up music

有意无意触动着心中的感觉

Stirs up feelings in heart consciously or unconsciously

独自悲伤的时候

When at the time falling into blue by self

是否还有人在远方应和

Whether there are echoes by a man at distance

Photo by: Zhao Crowley   摄影：向昭

《璇流》
SWIRLING FLOW

如一股璇流

Like a swirling flow

我坠入

I fell into

在流的中心空转

A center of a swirling flow and idling

迷失了方向

Lost my direction

无力自拔

Unable to pull out

任凭心事沉沦

Despite the fallen of mind

任凭自我失去

Despite the lost of self

或许是前世的宿缘

It may be the long cherished wish that comes from the past life

注定今生如此来还

It doomed to be returned like this in this life

我踏浪而行

I stepped on waves and go ahead

只听见自己的声音

Only, I can hear my own voice

和在风中回荡

Echoed to wind

我在岩石间跳跃

I am caprioling among rocks

与心对话

Chatting with heart

却听见坚强碎落的声音

But I heard the sound of broken down strength

随着涛声沉没

Fallen With sound of waves

只想在海底依靠

Only want to relay on depth of sea bottom

即使黑暗

Even it is dark

即使迷惘

Even it is at a loss

不识逃脱的迷径

Unknown the path of escaping

无边的荒漠

Endless desert

何曾有绿洲

Where is oasis?

《雨夜》
Rain Night

大雨滂沱的夜

Night, Pouring

没有星星和月亮

No star, No moon

路灯的光辉拖长了行人的影

Radiance of streetlights, Shades of peoples dragged long

在雨中纷飞

Flying in rain

车辆溅起的水花

Water flower splashed by vehicles

一朵朵

Blossom

于心中湿润

Wet heart

忽而凉忽而热

Suddenly cold suddenly hot

为这迷离无尽的黑暗

For the endless blurred darkness

幸而可以期待

Lucky there is expectation

172

明天的太阳

Sun of tomorrow

冲破云层

Will break through the cloudiness

将温暖细细洒落

Sparking the warmness slowly

无论阴云密布的口了有多久

Not matter how long the overcasting would last for

心存希望

Hopes in heart

使可支撑

Stand by the support

直到重展的笑颜

Until smile face re-shows

《无愁花》
WORRY – NOT-FLOWER

去远方吗？

Heading to distance?

别忘了带上我，带上诗

Don't forget to take me, take poems

心有尘埃的时候

When heart covered by dust

让我们开车去兜风

Let's go for a joyride

蓝天在上，白云悠悠

Blue sky is above, White cloud is long

看一湾湾水绕

Look bay water around

放下满心的愁烦

Put it down, the full heart of worries

滴清精神的污渍

Clear up dirt in spirit

返璞归真的简单

To be simple and returns to natural

让那些曾经的不堪与伤害远离

Let it go far away, the ever unbearable and hurts

自己选择的路不该有怨言

No compliant should be on the road chose by oneself

即使没有清风

Even there is no clear wind

用自己的双手也能抚平皱褶

Iron the wrinkle plain with own two hands

掬　掌清泉

Hold a hands full springs

润泽内心的荒芜

Moist the uncultivated inside of heart

种满一心无愁花

Grow a heart-bed of Worry-Not-Flower

你若盛开

If you bloom

清风自来

Clear breeze comes itself

Photo by: Zhao Crowley   摄影：向昭

《美女与野兽》

BEAUTY AND BEAST

野兽：

Beast:

曾经的伤害让我的心坚硬

The ever hurt harden my heart

冷酷带来野兽的命运

The grim take me into a weird of being beast

巫师的魔法将我笼罩

The magic of wizard shuts me in

我在冰封四季的寒冷里学习去爱

I am learning how to love in the cold of frozen four seasons

玻璃法灯下的玫瑰一片片的凋零

The rose under the magic glass light dying petals by petals

我的时间一分一秒的过去

My time passed by minute-by-minute and second-by-second

等待命运的救赎

Waiting for the salvation of destiny

等待深情的到来

Waiting for the come of beloved

美女：

Beauty:

乡间的田野雏菊盛开

Daisy blooms all over the country field

大自然的绿色润泽心田

Green of nature water the heart

在那森林的深处有一座古堡

There is an old castle in depth of the forest

古堡里住着外表可怕的野兽

An ugly appearance beast lives in the castle

厚重的皮毛下掩藏不住深情的双眼

Deep loves in his eyes cannot be hidden by thick heavy fur

当我们共舞

When we dance together

分明有那款款的深情融化冰寒

Shows clearly, a deep feeling unfroze the frozen ice

囚禁了的身体囚禁不住的爱情

Body can be prisoned but love cannot be

当这一切在现实中实现

When this realized in reality

热情可以化尽所有的冰霜

Enthusiasm would melt all frozen frosts

美好的时光指日可待

Good times just around the figure tips

巫师

Wizard

爱情不是想来就来想走就走

Love is not a game comes and goes at your thought

这是一份坚定的艺术

The is an art of firm

唯有心无杂陈

Only when your heart has no distractions

才可担当

It can take responsibilities

两心共舞

Until two hearts dancing together

才敢问世间情为何物

Dare to ask what love is

直教人生死相许

Make people promise life and death phrase

《清明祭》[8]

QING MING MEMORIAL

秋风托思异国月

Autumn breeze holds up miss under the moon of foreign land

春柳凭栏故乡云

Spring willow lean on railing with the cloud of home country

迢迢万里炎黄情

Wandering thousands of miles thought in Yanhuang feelings

芊芊芳草九州同

Flourishing grasses are the same in JiuZhou

清明时节忆汉祖

Remember ancestor of Han in this Qing Ming festival

雨落飞花慰秦心

Comfort hearts of Qin among the fallen rain and flying flowers

《离海那么近》
SO CLOSE TO SEA

离海那么近的城市有很多

There are so many cities so close to a sea

独爱的只有悉尼

But the only love I have is to Sydney

住在这里那么多年

Live in this city for so many years

熟悉了你的角角落落

I am used to its every corner

曼丽海边的柔风

Soft breeze of Manly beach

邦黛沙滩的落日

Golden sunset along the Bondi way

拉普洛斯湾的鸥鹭

Seagulls and herons of La Perouse

情人港的双影对对

And couples walking along the Darling Harbor

南半球的四月

The April of the southern hemisphere

又见红叶漫蓝山

Maple leaves red through the blue mountain again

只想不再徘徊

Do not want to wander again

错过这秋季的浪漫

And miss the romantic of season autumn

你来或着不来

Come or not come

我就在这里

I am here

你见或者不见

Meet or not meet

秋色的绚丽依样旖旎

The brilliant color of autumn would still be the same

《飞鸟与鱼》

A FLYING BIRD AND THE FISH

习惯了写诗

Used to write poems

便会用诗意的心情看世界

Then look at this world with poetical mood

看见天上的飞鸟

Seeing a flying bird on sky

想起与鱼的爱情

Recalled the love story of a flying bird and the fish

一个天上

One is on sky

一个洋底

One is at bottom of ocean

永远的俯瞰与仰望

Forever looks down and looks up

永远的游走与飞翔

Forever swim and flies

飞鸟的心鱼儿可曾懂

Would the fish understand the heart of a flying bird

鱼儿的不语飞鸟可感知

Would the flying bird sense the silence of a fish

飞鸟与鱼

A flying bird and the fish

共有一片蓝

Share the same piece of blue

一个在天空

One is on sky

一个在洋底

One is at bottom of the ocean

何处是交界

Where is the common border

或许在天边

It may be at the end of the sky

或许是洋的尽头

It may be at the end of the ocean

浩渺且无垠......

Mighty and boundless

《半个月亮》

HALF MOON

风再起时

When wind starts up again

半个月亮爬上树梢

Half moon climbed up to the top of a tree

坐在山巅

Sitting on top of a hill

你看着山脚下的万家灯火

Saw light of unlimited homes

秋风瑟瑟

"Shasha" of the Autumn wind

你裹紧了风衣

You pull tightly of the coat

对自己说"受过伤的人只爱自己"

And said to yourself "the hurt person only loves himself"

寒冷依然侵袭

Cold invaded as the same

太过自我的爱温度只有那么一点点

The temperature of self-love is only that a bit

高处不胜寒

Cold cannot be prevented at a very high level

如同被魔法囚禁的野兽

Like the beast prisoned in the magic jail

即使尊为王子的身躯

Even respected as a prince

不会爱的人也无法光芒万丈

The person who doesn't know how to love cannot shine out the radiant
light

你有一份理想

You have an ideal

征战四方成为王者

Campaign quartet to become a king

王者的胸怀应该可纳万民

Heart of king should be able to tolerant people

用太阳的温度普照天下

Having the temperature of sun to illuminate all things

王者的战争也会有败

There could be lost battle of kings' wars

王者的心却从来不会屈服

The heart of king, however, could never be surrender

月儿一半的时候

When the moon is in half

静心待月圆

Waiting for a full moon with a quiet heart

月满之时

When the moon becomes as a full moon

野兽应该学会勇敢去爱

The beast would be able to love bravely

立地方成王

Down to the earth to be a king

《大爱无疆》
BIG LOVE WITH NO LIMIT

你看，天那么广阔

See, how broad the sky is

因为无界

Because of no limit

鸟儿才能自由地飞翔

Birds can fly freely

飞的高远

Fly lofty

你看，海那么壮阔

See, how broad the sea is

因为无际

Because of no limit

鱼儿才能畅快地远游

Fishes can swim freely

游到深遂

Swim deeply

大爱无疆

Big love with no limit

不因他人的瑕疵

No hate defect of the others

不忌他人的过失

Not bear grudge fault of the others

因心而爱

Love from heart

才能宽厚

Can be lenient

爱无涯

Love with no limit

方可拓疆土

Can open up territory

统全局

Then command the whole situation

《红豆沙》

RED BEAN PASTE

我用把红豆熬成沙的火

Cook on fire, I am making red bean paste

细细地熬心

Heart boiling, slowly-slowly

温火煲出的汁液

Mild temperature, slow fire, juicing out

如溪水潺潺

Like a creek babbling

在心田间漫溢

Overflowing, fill whole field of heart

树梢的鸟儿叽喳

Chirping up, birds at top of trees

和着一曲相思

Chime in a song of miss

池塘偶有蛙鸣

Singing occasionally, frogs in pond

回荡出满池猗涟

Echo, stir up full pond ripples

热闹也独独是它们的

Noisy, only for them

红豆在心火间沸腾

Ebullience, the red bean cooked by fire of heart

悄悄地

Quietly

沙沙地

Rustle

轻语呢喃成沙的缠绵

Lingeringly, whispered into paste

静静地

Tranquilly

默默地

Silently

煎熬满满的沙弥

Tormented into full paste

注入蜜糖的甜

Pouring sweet of honey

融合豆香的涩

Melting puckery in red bean

细细地熬心的火

The fire boiling the heart slowly-slowly

我把红豆熬成一世的沙

I boil the red beans into a century's paste

一世漫溢的思念

A century's overflowing miss

《蓝》
BLUE

天上来的那一缕

Comes from sky, that piece

散落进凡间谷地

Scattered into the mortal ordinary world

蓝了溪水

Blue into creeks

蓝了枝叶

Blue into leaves

蓝了个漫山遍野

Blue into whole fields and mountains

轻轻地游走

Gently swam away

慢慢地晕开

Softly halo opened

蓝透满山的相思

Blue into the miss cover all over the mountain

蓝进山谷间回应

Blue into the echoes among valleys

眺望回眸

Looking up and looking back

我于这蓝色间寻觅

I am searching among the blues

寻觅山天一色的默契

Looking for the harmony of sharing same color by mountain and sky

寻觅浅淡深蓝的心事

Looking for the light or dark blue hide in heart

觅见你在暗蓝中深藏

Find you hiding among the dark blue

用你不露声色的包容

Your not bat an eyelid tolerance

换我心若天蓝的广阔

Exchanged my heart blue broad

Photo by: Zhao Crowley　　　摄影：向昭

《真》
TRUTH

牡丹艳丽

Peony gorgeous

玫瑰芬芳

Rose fragrance

雏菊淡雅

Daisies Elegant

松兰高洁

Pine and orchid noble

自由的世界里

In a free world

真实地活着

Alive in truth

绽放自我

Self-blooming

淡定从容

Calm and leisurely

黄河的水黄

Water in the yellow water is yellow

长江的道弯

Road along the long river is zig-zag

喜马拉雅雪莲高冷

Snow lotus of Himalayas are high and cold

马里亚纳珊瑚灿烂

Corals of Mariana are magnificent

真实就是一种自然状态

Truth is a natural status

无须掩藏

No need to hide

仓央嘉措[9]说，

Zangyang Gyatso, the fifth Dalai Lama of Tibet says in his poem

你来或者不来

Come or not come

情就在那里

Feelings are there

我说

I said

你真或者不真

True or not true

岁月自有答案

Answer inside of times

《老歌》

AN OLD SONG

播一首老歌

An old song

在午夜的暗里

Comes out of a radio in this dark midnight

感受忧伤

Feel blue

暗哑的嗓音

Dull voice

吟唱着爱情

Sing for love, but,

却不再是年轻的模样

Not the appearance of young

曾经的沧桑

The ever vicissitudes

幻灭了热情的悸动

Disillusioned the throbbing of enthusiasm

和不出悦人的小夜曲

Unable to echo a pleasing serenade

只有月色彷徨

Hover left in this moonlight

彷徨、迷惘、阻滞的步伐

Hover, at a loss, blocked steps

患得、患失，苍老而至的容颜

Worried about obtain, worried about loss, hoary face appears

倦了、累了、爱不起的灵魂

Weary, tired, unable -t o -love soul

却又不甘

Yet, not resigned to

沉沦的心分明还有舞动

Dance, still lives in a fallen heart

随附老歌的音符

With the rhythm of this old song

缓缓中藏匿了深情

Deep-love hides in slowness

那一首老歌

That old song

在心底唱了十数载

Sing at the bottom of heart for decade

终究还是爱情的模样

After All, it is appearance of love

不再有少年的热忱

Enthusiasm of young is no longer there

满荷的却是年轮的味道

Flavor of year rings fully loaded

深沉而久远

Deep and faraway

《远方的诗》
POEM OF DISTANCE

把生活过成一首诗

Live life like a poem

在烛光里浪漫

Fill romance in candlelight

虽然不能免去苟且

Although worries cannot be avoid

至少给白己一段时光

At lease granting self a period of time

在美酒中沉醉

Drunk in fine wines

让月影洒进浓汤

Moonlight spreads into cream soup

将星光揉碎于家常便饭

Roll starlight into ordinary home meal

滋养心灵的成长

Nutrition growth of heart

沉心于静谧

Sink heart into quietness

专注于美味

Concentrate the delicious

让平淡的日子盈满情调

Let the ordinary days fill full of sentiment

《心魔》

DEMON OF HEART

心魔多多少少

Demon of heart here and there

爱的时候只说don't care

Being in love but says "don't care"

尊严要用对峙表现

Dignity shows up via confrontation

想念的时候却无法温柔

Miss, but cannot be soft

相爱容易相处难

Easy to fall in love, hard to get along

自由的灵魂象风一样

The free soul like the wind

渴望相拥却漂泊不停留

Desire for embrace, unable to stop wandering life

想说一声"嗨，你好吗！"

Wish to say "Hi，how are you"

出口却成"你走吧"

Words came out and changed to "Let you go"

牵挂也分离

Care but separate

拿起电话的手按下停止拨出的健

Phone be picked up, fingers stopped to dial

空荡的心里装满了醉的酒

Dunking wine filled heart full

懂得的心却敌不过一张伤人的嘴

Understandable-heart unable to win a hurting mouth

不想问为什么

Do not want to ask why

流动的空气里一场僵持的局

Flowing air holds a stalemate party

想要的幸福败给傲骄

The desired happiness lose to pride

笑容掩藏了泪水

The smiling face covered by tears

爱的心说着don't care

Being in love but says "DO NOT CARE"

《勇敢的心》
BRAVE HEART

风笛

Bagpipe

在旷野中穿行

Penetrate through the broad field

绿色

Green

铺满整个草原

Covered the whole grassland

战火

War fire

纷飞在沙场

Fly over the battlefield

心爱的人

The beloved

送你一朵茉莉芳香

Send you the fragrance of a jasmine

颤抖

Trumble

整颗心的律动

The bump of the whole heart

荣光

Hornor

为着自由的天空

Pursue a free sky

战马

Warhorse

嘶鸣在疆场

Hoar over the battlefield

逐爱的心

A heart pursuing love

在锥痛中成长

Grow up in the pain

抛头颅、洒热血的气概

The spirit of casting head and sprinkling blood

换取一世的春满家园

Exchange the century spring of homeland

此岸、彼途

This shore, that way

跨越了心河的艰难

Cross over the hard of heart river

静待七叶花开

Waiting for the bloom of seven-leaves-flower in the silent

《心殇》

DEATH OF MINORS HEART

咬着牙

Biting the teeth

吞着痛

Swallowing the pain

在沉默中隐忍

Forbearance in silence

我听见心脏一厘一厘撕碎的声音

I heard the sound of heart tearing center meters by center meters

曾经的深情放在眼前

The ever deep-love is at the front

却是双手无法触碰的距离

But it is an unable-touch distance

含笑的双眼

Smiles in eyes

滴血的内心

Blood in heart

曾几何时

Since when

从熟悉到陌生

From familiar with becomes as strangers

走了那么漫长的路

Walked in a so long road

却只用了短暂的时间

But it is in such a short time

已经记不起上次是在什么时候

Unable to remember, when it was that

见过你毫无隐藏纯真的笑脸

I saw your pure smiling face with no mask

那些无暇的往事

All the non-defect stories in the past

何时就飘散在了风里

When it was buried in the wind and gone

涤荡了青春的勇敢

Washed the brave of youth away

沉淀为成熟的静默

Sink into the silence of mature

在无息无语的时光里

In the time passed quietly

蹉跎着一往情深

Lost the dearest love as the time goes by

《枫叶红时》

WHEN MAPLE LEAVES TURN INTO RED

枫叶红时

When maple leaves turn into red

我在秋天里等你

I will wait for you in autumn

漫天铺地的红

Red is all over the sky and earth

红了心头的念

Reds the miss of heart

念去春天里的风

Miss the gone of spring breeze

吹在枝头上的新绿

Taking away the new green of branches

念记夏天里的雨

Miss the rain of summer

洗涤皓天上的湛蓝

Washing away the boundless blues in sky

念来秋天中的果

Miss the fruits of autumn

沉淀春耕夏培的辛劳

Memory the toil of spring plow and Sumer foster

捡一叶的绯红

Picking up a leave's red

羞怯满心的柔情

Blushful the fondness of full heart

放一湖之碧水

Let it go with the green water of the lake

深藏了一往情深的等待

Hiding deeply the dearest-love into the wait

等在秋天里

Wait in autumn

飘零落霞菲红的枫叶

Wait until the maple leaves turn into red

Photo by: Zhao Crowley　　　摄影：向昭

《待》

WAITING

秋叶尽落

Autumn leaves lag off

冬起寒凉

Winter cold starts up

独对西窗

Facing west window alone

淡河瘦月

Small river, slim moon

小舟浅横

Little boat sidelong the shallow

野渡鹭影

Heron shades covers the wild field

何不成双

Why not in a couple

唏嘘慨叹

Sigh sighed

具付时光

All hand over to time

任意蹉跎

Let it be as time goes by

蛙静蛐默

Frogs keep silent, crickets in quiet

虫蛰无惊

Insects hibernating with no disturbing

待望春光

Wait until spring comes

《重归诗心》

POETRY HEART RETURNS

周末的夜色里

In the night light of a weekend

独守一个人的寂

Guard self's loneliness alone

喧嚣褪去

All the noise's gone

寻找渐消的诗意

Looking for the eventually – disappeared poetry heart

繁华落尽

When all the prosperous gone

看硝烟之后的迷雾

Look through the misty of smoke from guns

西风曾起的战事

The war started up by the west wind

碎将明媚初心

Broke down the bright initial-heart into pieces

楚雄知是谁

Who is the hero of Chu

又何如

What does that a matter

泛舟江心

Rafting boat in the center of river

浪淘尽

Waves washed away all

潇潇雨歇

Rain stops

不如归隐

It would be better to hermit

归隐山林一色

Hermit in the colors of mountains and forests

放心于自由

Place the heart into freedom

远离纷争锁心

Keep a distance, away from disputes

独醒于天涯

Wake leisurely at the boundary of the world

《致生命》

TO LIFE

翦翦的秋风吹过

Gentle mild autumn breeze through

南太平洋的海水泛起波澜

Starting up the waves along waters of the southern Pacific Ocean

千帆的港湾静谧安详

Harbor is quiet and serene with lots sails

离海那么近的城热闹喧杂

The city close to the sea is so busy and noisy

一个人在这两重间穿行

I by myself walk between the dual

自由的涟漪于心间荡漾

Free waves undulate in heart

夕阳的余辉铺满海面

Afterglow of sunset covers the whole surface of the sea

孩子们的嬉笑在波光间跳跃

Laughs of children leap over the waves

散落进水面如精灵忽隐忽现

Sparking into the water, like elves flickering up and down

阳光照耀驱散阴霾

Sunlight shines and get the haze away

如母亲的怀抱温暖和煦

Like the hug of a mother, warm and gentle

洋流的彼岸曾是我生命源起的地方

The other side shore is the origin place of my life

行走过的年轮记载了往事

Walk through and year rings left, recorded stories of past

蹉跎过的岁月不再回首

Won't look back to the times, when it passed away

遥致未来的律动

Remotely greeting to the hope of future

外面的世界很精彩

The outside world is brilliant

只愿生命的余晖熠熠光耀

Only wish light of life shining out

《友情就酒》
FRIENDSHIP TOAST WITH WINE

你来或者不来

Come or not come

美味就在这里

The gourmet is here

酒杯高举

Rise up wine glass

下肚就是深情

Cheer up for friendship

绿叶为舟

Green leaves are boat

扇贝遨游

Scallop swim inside

就当胡萝卜丝是彩鱼

Carrots are colorful fish

心火烤熟白菜和虾

Toast white cabbage and prawns in fire of heart

闺蜜俩的吃吃喝喝

Two close girlfriends eating and drinking

友情就酒

Friendship with wines

越吃越有

There would be more and more

《泾渭》[10]

BOUNDARY OF JING-WEI RIVER

往古之时

Trace back to the ancient time

天地混沌

The world is a chaos

积重难返

Heavy accumulated, hardly to return

柔情无在

No exist of tenderness

天不兼覆

Heaven is not covered

地不周载

Earth is not loaded

星月无分

No separate of moon and stars

昼夜无差

No difference of days and nights

盘古[11]开天

Pan Gu opened the sky

方辟鸿蒙

He starts the very beginning of the world

女娲[12]炼石

Fairy Nuwa refine stones

五色补天

Five colors patch up the sky

止暧昧

Stopped the ambiguous

分界限

Boundaries the limit

风清云白

Wind is clear and clouds are white

天地永固

Sky is firmed and earth keeps forever

日月星辰

Sun, moon, star and time

各司其职

Operate their own functions

心澈灵轻

Heart is limpid and soul is light

方行久远

Then longer – forever lasts

《燕归巢》

SWALLOW RETURNS TO NEST

春来衔泥筑家巢

When spring comes, hold mud in mouth to build nest

燕栖云水间

Swallows live in the place between sky and water

秋去南飞觅温暖

When autumn ends, fly to south for warmth

燕戏冬寒意

Swallows play the winter cold

燕去燕儿归

Swallows come and swallows go

只问春雨冬雪

Depend on the rain of spring and snow of winter

花开花儿谢

Flowers bloom and flowers fell

唯依夏炙秋凉

Relay on the hot of summer and cool of autumn

226

《勿忘我》

FORGET–ME-NOT

当一切等待成空茫

When all the waiting became an empty

吾心培净土

Clean mud in heart

栽一株勿忘我

Plant a forget-me-not

柔情化为花间紫

Melt tenderness into purple of flowers

静开在心底

Bloom quietly at the bottom of heart

不必问我去哪里

Do not ask, where I am going to

是否还归来

If I will come back

年年岁岁花相似

Flowers are similar in each year

只需记取这一抹

The one to remember, is this unique

一抹花间紫

This purple among flowers

风亦吹亦远

Wind gone further and further

云逾飞逾淡

Cloud flies lighter and lighter

不再留恋

No longer nostalgia

用这一抹尘封

Seal the memory with this flower

用这紫色记取

Memorial the past with this purple

封尘埃卑微的失我

Seal lost-me in the humble dust

记紫色绚烂的傲我

Recall pride-me in the brilliant purple

我就是我

I am I

无改的初心

No change of the initial-heart

随云走

Gone with cloud

228

随风飞

Fly with wind

不必问去了哪里

No need to ask, where I am going to

不必问是否还归来

No need to ask, if I will come back

Photo by: Zhao Crowley　　摄影：向昭

《天蓝·海蓝》
SKY-BLUE, SEA-BLUE

分不清那样的一片蓝

Unable to tell if that piece of blue

是海还是天

Belongs to sea or sky

分不清远海的一点白

Unable to tell if that white of the distance – sea, is

是鸥还是帆

A seagull or a sail

我们在海边行走

We are walking along the coast of the sea

任凭海风吹拂

Let the wind of sea breeze on face

吹起波涛汹涌的海浪

Breeze starts up stormy waves

吹进心底复苏的自我

Blow into heart and wake up oneself

吹化淤积了一个世纪的冰寒

Blow away icy cold accumulated a century

面朝大海的蓝

Facing the blue of the sea

心暖花开的暖

Warmed by blooming of heart flower

别让微尘覆盖了骄傲

Don't let the dust cover the pride

看着幸福渐行渐远

Seeing off happiness walking away further and further

敞开胸怀拥抱海天一色的蓝

Open mind to hug the blue of sea and sky

我们在海边行走

We are walking along the seacoast

走进分不清是海还是天的蓝

Unable to tell if the blue belongs to sea or sky

《彼岸花》

FLOWER OF THE OTHER SIDE

彼岸花

Flower of the other side

开到荼蘼

Bloom up to extravagant

泣血的鲜红

Tears blood the fresh red

为谁怜

For whom it feels pity

彼岸花

Flower of the other side

曼陀罗华

Flower of Manta-Luo

虐洁的纯白

Oppressive pure white

为谁留

For whom it keeps

彼岸花

Flower of the other side

无义草莽

No meaning wilderness

掩心的艳蓝

Brilliant-blue of hiding heart

为谁忙

For whom it is busy

彼岸、此岸

This side, that side

生死了望

Watching between alive and death

江河隔

Divided by rivers

明一畔、暗一畔

Bright on this side, dark on that side

华之绝美

Flowery beautiful

伤断肠

Hurt till heartbroken

《彼此经年》
SEVERAL YEARS PASSED BY

那一年

That year

穿过广场

Pass by the ground

火热的夏风飞扬

Hot wind of summer flied upward

撩起青春的发丝

Lifting up hairs of youth

为自由而轻翔

Flying lightly for freedom

这一年

This year

走过小径

Walking beside the path

萧瑟的秋风冷寂

Bleak wind of autumn cools down alone

吹落记忆的红叶

Blowing down red leaves of memory

为纪念而落殇

Death fallen to memory

那一年

That year

热血沸腾

Passionate boiled up

为着理想奋不顾身

Fight for ideals with no fear

终却遥无可及

Out of reach at the end

一如划过天空的流星

Like a meteor passing by sky

耀眼却奔赴沧桑

Brightness but towards to vicissitudes

这一年

This year

理性淡漠

Different to ideal

为着归隐更姓埋名

Change name to hermit

竟是采菊东篱

Picking flowers of east fence

仿若飘零树间之红叶

Like maple leaves fallen among branches

殷红而融土为泥

Blood red and melt into mud

那一年、这一年

That year, this year

同一个我

Same me

彼时于北、此刻而南

That year at north, this moment in south

同一颗心

Same heart

经年的张扬，归寂的隐忍

Several years' fly-by, return forbearance of loneliness

同路殊途

Same road different future

那一年，曾经年轻

That year, ever-young

这一年，不惮初老

This year, not afraid of being old

《音符的岁月》
YEARS OF MUSIC NOTE

每一个音符的穿透

Penetrate of each music note

越过岁月的年轮

Cross over years' year-rings

我看见韶华的容颜

I saw the face of good years

在指尖上的跳跃

Leap over the finger tips

记忆的深处

Deep inside of memories

第一次柔情的苏醒

The first tenderness waken up

沙滩漫步的双影

Walking along beach, shades of couple

那是爱情的感觉

Feeling of love

朦胧也热烈

Twilight but passionate

象音符的跳动

Like the leaps of music notes

忽而水润

Water stream suddenly

忽而山岳

Hill top suddenly

忽而悲伤

Suddenly blueness

忽而欢畅

Suddenly happiness

一直地流淌

Flows ahead non-stopping

如清泉甜润

Sweet like clear springs

如烈火熊熊

Flaming like raging fire

在沉寂的生命里燃烧

Burning in silent lonely life

燃烧最后的想念

Burnt the last miss

浴火重生

Rise from ashes

即使沧桑了容颜

Although vicissitudes the face

也无法沧桑跃动的灵魂

Unable to vicissitudes the leaping soul

音符的岁月里

In the years of music notes

相见不如怀念

To cherish rather than to meet

--------2017.6.5 理查德.克莱德曼音乐会随想

---------Wrote for the concert of Richard Clydeman in Sydney on 5th

June 2017

《北海北》
NORTH OF NORTH SEA

我想背起行囊

Pack up luggage

追逐我的梦想

Pursuing my dream

追随自己的真心

Follow up a true heart

去浪迹天涯

Wandering around the world

我想丢弃所有的过往

I want to throw away all the past

不在一成不变中死亡

Rather than dying in the no-change

我想让微风轻拂脸庞

I grant breeze to touch my face

也在暴雨中狂奔怒吼

Allow storm rushing madly and roaring wildly

我想有风和日丽的静好

I wish to have tranquil moment in a gentle beautiful day

也想有风雪交加的疼痛

I am not afraid of cold-pains in snow neither

我想这就是活着的感觉

In those I feel alive

我不知道我的生命会有多久

I don't know how long my life would last

但至少我不想在沉寂中无知无觉

But I don't want to live unconsciously in silence

我想行走天涯

I hope to walk and reach the boundary of sky

找到我自己

Found myself

看见自己欢笑

See my laugh

也看见自己流泪

See my tear

我想在行走的旅途

On the journey

碰到同行的你

I wish to meet you, you will come along with me

可以懂我喜欢的风景

You appreciate the scenes I like

可以和我一起

You can be with me

在活着的感觉里经历山高水长

In the alive feels, we experience the height of mountains

and length of water

《别后愿无恙》
WISH WELL AFTER THE GOODBY

路的尽头

At the end of a road

我们筋疲力尽

We are exhausted

带着满身的荆棘和伤痕

Thorns and scars are full of body

在相遇的丨字路口

At the cross of the road, we met

互相问候

Greeting to each other

声音变的小心翼翼

Voice changed into carefulness

怕是惊飞了枝头的鸟儿

Afraid of terrified away birds on tree branches, and

日后再也寻不到踪迹

Unable to find their trace later

是什么改变了曾经的无猜

What it is that changed the Ever-No-Guess

让流动的空气僵持屏息

Made the flow air deadlock breath

是谁偷走了当时的欢颜

Who it is that steals the happy face of that moment

让往事随风成了空空的梦境

Let the past story became an empty dream

你不说、我正好不问

You don't want to say, I am happily not to ask

倨傲成为一条界河

Pride becomes a boundary of a river

波澜不惊只有暗流涌动

Placid but with undercurrent surging

河面印出两双笑面

Smile faces of a couple was printed on the surface of the river

只当从未发生

Take it as never happened

此时平常

It is just ordinary at this moment

只想淡淡地问一声"你好吗"？

Plainly ask, "How are you"

此去流年，别后愿无恙

Gone from now on, wish well after the goodbye

Photo by: Zhao Crowley　　摄影：向昭

《忘记》
FORGET

忘记

Forget

只用了一霎那的时间

Only costs a second

看着你慢慢消失

Saw your disappearance slowly

沉没在地平线的尽头

Sink at the end of the horizon

冬天的冷也穿透衣襟

Coldness of winter penetrates through my coat

寒进心里

Goes inside of heart

可依然要欢笑

Still, need to keep happy laugh

大声到不露痕迹

Keep laugh loudly until no mark shows out

如果这样可以让你走的没有心痛

If it could make you go with no pain of heart

一场离别的盛宴何尝不可欢歌笑语

Why could not the party of farewell be filled with songs and laugh

悲伤只不过是虚假的祭奠

Sadness only a memorial of fake

用短暂的时光流尽永远的泪

Running out of forever-tears in a so short time

然后呢

Then/After?

就是忘记

forget

一笔一笔地减除

Eliminating a bit by bit

直到无形

Until non

成为明天的故事

Turn in stories of tomorrow

《人生若只如初见》
IF LIFE LIKES THE FIRST GLANCE

心，也有倦意的时候

Heart, has moment to feel tired

看过了人情冷暖

Seen all the coldness and warmness of human feelings

只愿记住云卷云舒

Wish to remember open-cloud and close-cloud

天上飘过的

The one flight pass of sky

或是昨日的那朵

Whether it is the one of yesterday's

只是形状已任意了变幻

It is only the shape that changed

更改的模样不再依旧

The changed appearance is no longer the same of before

情，也有困顿的时候

Love, has moment to feel wearied

走过了路短路长

Walked all the way, either long or short

只是想起一年复一年

Remember year after year

曾经的故地

The Ever-Old-Haunt

还是那片长浪白沙

Whether it is still that long waves and white sands

或是旧迹已随性了淹没

Previous marks are already been covered randomly

消弭的欢颜再难寻觅

The disappeared happy face is no longer be able to find

河，晨雾氤氲的时候

River, at the foggy mist morning

静静地鸟飞鱼游

Quietly, river birds fly，lake fish swims

可曾追溯源来源往

Whether traced back the origin and root

做一只水鸟吧

Wish to be a river bird

或静守岁月的安然

Or to guard peace of days quietly

或游曳漫湾的悠闲

Or to tour drag leisure of a half bay

不曾知道岁月的沧桑

Never known vicissitudes of time

只相约守一世初见的笑容

Only, promise to keep smiles of a century first-glance

和谐了时光

Harmony time

如此便好

It is just good

----佳维斯湾水云间

------Wrote at the Jarvis Bay on 2nd July 2017

Photo by: Zhao Crowley　　　摄影：向昭

《海》
THE SEA

还是喜欢这片海

Like this sea

总也看不够的惊涛拍岸

Unable to see enough, that storms beat its shore

那一片

That piece

蓝到深刻的忧伤

Blue deeply until to the sadness

却也停不下地流动

Unable to stop flow yet

突破窄窄的峡湾

Break through the shallow fjord

进入更广的洋流

Enter into the broader ocean current

如果遭遇暖风

If met with warm wind

那一瞬就救赎了冰寒

Icy-cold be saved at that moment

搅起热浪滔天

Stir up hot waves hitting the sky

那一片

That piece

也不惧怕凄冷的蓝

Never afraid of the blue of coldness

冲撞上冰山

Clashed with ice burg

也可立时冰冻

Could be frozen immediately

用高冷的姿态傲视

Look down to a cold pride posture

冰火两重天

Ice-fire fairy tales

都是生命的力量

They are all strength of life

看尽喜怒哀乐

Look through all emotions

激情地翻涌

Passion still surging

就是这一片海

It is this piece of the sea

总也看不够的

Never be seen enough

风平浪静抑或激流涌动

Calm down or rush surging

《诗和远方》
POEMS AND DISTANCE

这一场说走就走的旅行

The travel by my whims

只为心的放飞

Just for letting heart go

剪断缠缠绕绕的负累

Cut off burdens of harassing

不看绝途的磕磕绊绊

Not afraid of obstacles on road

曾经的那场风花雪月

The ever-romance, whether-

是否红尘梦中缘

It is a red dust destiny in dream

不问何忧

Never ask what to worry

不问前程

Never ask where is future

只问浅笑是否心安然

Only ask if the light smile is at rest

行囊里装进鼓鼓缦缦

Drumming luggage

丢弃不掉现实里的苟且

Unable to throw away the good-for-nothing in reality

至少可以奔赴远方的花香诗意

At least, be able to go for fragrance of flower and poem of distance

暂且的逃离

The temporary escape

但愿行一场治愈的奔忙

Only wish it is a curable busy

不能擦干所有的泪流满面

Unable to wipe off all the tears running down the face

也可得一段欢愉雀跃的暂时忘记

At least, be able to have a temporary-forgot and happy for the moment

行走在山水之间

Walking among views of mountains and water

让我们体验归真反璞的初世

Let's experience the beginning of the whole nature

《等到那时风淡云轻》

TILL THE CLOUD GENTLED AND BREEZE SOFTEN

等到那时风淡云轻

Till the cloud gentled and breeze soften

我已经忘了

I forgot already, that

来时的路上

On the coming road

我们曾经追逐

We ever chased each other

追逐月光里的音符

Chased music notes in moonlights

梦里低吟小夜曲

Whispering serenade in dreams

追逐星图下的画笔

Chased drawing pens under stars

填满心间的亏缺

Filling up deficit of heart

我曾经轻舞罗袖

I ever lighting danced red sleeves

曼妙诗曲

Wrote pomes, compose music gracefully

你也曾夜色催更里默默

You have ever been quiet in the nightlight changing

平抚伤痕

Comfort the hurt

追逐里太多的玩闹

There is too much play in the chasing

却惊失了距离

Even mind-blow lost distance

何时里就迷失了方向

It was when that we lost the direction

我在花间

I am in flowers

你却迷在林里

You are at the forest

是否还能握住我的手

Whether you can hold my hands like before

带我重回初途

Take me back to the original way

《夜色霓虹》

NEON COLORED NIGHT

夜色霓虹

Neon colored night

冬末的寒凉里

In cold of the end of winter

依看QVB门前的雕塑

Stand by and watching the status in front of QVB

何吋起

When it was from that

市政厅的大楼竟有了霓虹的彩光

The building of the Town Hall gets the color lights of neon

有多久

How long it was since

没有注视过这样的夜色繁华

Last time I gazed the bustling in this night light

我忘了时间

I forgot time

也陡然想起好久没有写诗

Suddenly remembered, it was for a long time that I didn' t write any poem

总是挣扎在情绪的漩涡里

Struggling in the eddy of mood all the time

诗意的灵魂好象跌入了夜色的暗

It seems that the poetic soul has fallen into the darkness of night

找不到出口

Unable to find the exit

有多久断裂在时光的流逝里

Hot long it was that broke in the pass of time

寻不到你的踪迹

Unable to find footmark of you

我也学会一点点的忘记

I learnt to forget bit by bit eventually

忘记臆想中的温暖

Forget the warmness of illusion

学会一个人的坚强

Learnt to be strong by myself

春天快要到了吗

Would spring come soon

枝头有嫩绿的新芽

There are tender greens of new shoots on top of branches

悉尼的冬天本不寒冷

Winters of Sydney are not so cold

为何还是想念

Why miss is still there

春天的阳光

The sunlight of spring

许是那繁花灿烂

May bring the brilliant bloom, which

会让灵魂冲破忧伤

Could take soul to break through sadness

如你所许

As you wished

十里桃花

Ten miles of peach blossom

远离凡尘

Keep away from all dust

《相守相忘》

REMEMBER AND FORGET

那惊鸿一瞥

It was that glimpse when I saw you

注定了这样的相遇

Doomed the meet like this

让住进心里的爱情再也走不掉

Love roots in heart and unable to escape any more

不求与你的相守

No beg to accompany with each other

就算行走在寂寞里

Even walking in loneliness

也会花开在心底

Flowers would bloom at the bottom of heart

雨落的声音

The rhythm of fallen rains

静静聆听

Listen quietly

落花流水也是化入泥

Fallen flowers flowing water melted in mud

带一份馨香

With fragrance

不求相近

No beg to be close

只是想念那曾经的拥抱

Only because of missing the ever-hug, which

在我孤独的心里平添的温暖

Adds warmness in my lonely heart

错误的时间

At wrong time

遇见对的爱情

Encountered the right love

只能相望相忘

Only gaze and to forget

舍不得离开的

The leave unwilling to go

是心的软弱

It was the weakness of the heart

狠狠的能伤的

The one can be hurt hardly

是脆弱的自尊

It is the self-esteems of weakness

下不了手尘封的

The one unable to seal

是曾经的用心

It is the diligently of ever

指尖颤抖划过你的名字

Shaking fingers move cross over your name

加过又减过

Deleted / Added back / Again and Again

相望相忘吧

Remember and forget

只是因为爱情

All because of love

Photo by: Zhao Crowley   摄影： 向昭

《春时极光》

AURORA IN SPRING

繁花盛开的时候

When flowers bloom

就是春天了吗

Did spring come

可为何还有冬的残凉

But why there is still cold of winter

或许是心还未解冻

May it because the heart is still frozen

依旧等待温暖的信栈

Still wait for a letter of warm

好似绿荫葱茏

It likes the green-covers

静待时光

Waiting for a quiet - good moment comes

听说春天的气息

It was said that the breath of spring

带着极光

Brings the aurora

苍穹之下的星光

Star light under sky

也会格外明朗

Would be much brighter

想约你共享

Wish to have a date with you

不负这光阴的荏苒

Not to disappoint the time being

却又凭空对月

Yet watching moon on the sky

慨叹心河难知

Sigh whom it is that would understand this heart

流淌的清泉

The running springs

诉说谁的心语

Whose heart it is that whispering its language

蓝天碧海

Blue sky blue sea

伊人何在

Where is her

花开有期

Blooming flowers have time

灿烂一时

Brilliant is only in a moment

莫悔花谢流殇

Don't regret that if missing

绚丽难再

Beauty is no longer there

《撩春》
TEASING SPRING

一树桃红撩春色

Pink of peach in a tree teases spring

湖鸭静平卧

Lake ducks lie smoothly on water surface

江风轻摇芦苇荡

River breeze shakes the reeds softly

彩舟沙堤斜

Color boats titled on the sands beach

鹭啼枯枝知冬尽

Egret sings off the winter, dried branches know

暖阳渡水蓝

Warm sun crosses over the blue water

《何处待月圆》

WHERE TO WAIT FOR A FULL MOON

明月何处有

Where is the bright moon

把酒问青天

Rising up wine to ask blue sky

一世静心待

Waiting of a century in a peaceful heart

月缺也曾圆

The moon is ever-half and ever-full

悲欢离合聚

Sadness /Joyful /Separate/ Reunion

万事皆凭缘

All relay on fate

异国海边浪

Waves alongside seacoast on foreign land

他乡赏月时

When appreciating the moon on the others' hometown

邀舞沙共踏

Inviting beach sands for dancing

对影双自成

Seeing a couple shadows of self and the moon

《但愿人长久》

WISH COUPLES LAST LONG

月满的时候

At the time of full moon

是否可以忘了心缺的痛

Whether could forget the pain of loss heart

异乡的花好月圆里

Pretty flower and full moon time of the foreign land

独酌思念的寂

Alone, drink loneliness of miss

推杯换盏的祝福

Toast the cheers among people

只剩谁在风中萧然

Who was left in the wind wistful

但愿人长久

Wish couples last long

抬头望皓月

Look up the bright moon

对影两无言

Facing each other's shadow with no word

佳节的气氛

Atmosphere of the festival

是否可以不念漂泊的难

Whether could forget the hard of leading a wondering life

背井的离愁别绪里

Displease emotion in drifting

唯品思亲的寞

By self, taste the loneliness of homesick

明月升起的天涯

At the world end bright full moon rises

此时微浪苍茫的海角

The minor waves vastly at the corner of sea

千里共婵娟

Appreciate moon together thousand miles away

满月西梢头

Full moon is at the west branch top

金樽祝团圆

Take golden bottles up to toast a reunion

----------------2017年10月4日中秋节[13]

----------------Wrote for the Moon Festival on 4th Oct 2017

《馨香》

FRAGRANT

退潮的时候

At the time of ebb

海水是否能够听见浪哭的声音

Whether could the sea hear the crying of waves

雨打的时候

At the time of beating by rain

花儿是否能够感觉撕裂的痛楚

Whether could flowers feel the pain of tearing

爱着的时候

At the time of falling in love

心意是否能有足够坚持的理由

Whether could the heart strong enough to keep on going

尊严受挫的时候

At the time of dignity being foiled

高傲是否能够退让给绵绵温柔

Whether could the pride give way to the lasting tenderness

忽然之间的明白

The suddenly understood

默默无语里的点点滴滴

Bit by bit in the silence

不是让脚步渐行渐远

Not to let the foot walking further and further

而是在磨难的光阴里

But in the difficulty time

让心慢慢地靠近

To enable the heart to be closer and closer

等待情绪的沉淀

Waiting for the sink of emotion

在一份懂得里沐浴淡淡不断的馨香

In an understood to shower the faint fragrant constantly

《冥想》

MEDITATION

放空心情

Let the mood goes into empty

我只想在时光里发呆

I only wish to be in a daze at this moment

把记忆沉淀成一份冥想

Deposit memories into a meditation

在悠悠的静寂中回归自我

Return to myself in a leisure peace

不为情绪困扰

Not bounded by emotions

笑付沧桑的过往

Give the past to vicissitudes in laughing

看见那人那事那些岁月

Seen that person that thing in that year

默守这心这意这些蹉跎

Keep this heart this mind quietly in this idle away

也曾计较得失

Ever concerned the loss and gain

也曾不忘初心

But never forget the initial-heart

只是当种种渐渐成为习惯

When all these became a habit eventually

经历过的再难惹痛心扉

All the experience could no longer provoke pain of heart

收拾一地的碎落

Packing up trivial on the floor

即使伤痕累累

Even the wound is every where

也能在空放的心情里继续微笑

Let smiles keep in the empty mind

《又是一季蓝花楹》
JACARANDA SEASON RETURNS

又是一季蓝花楹

Jacaranda season returns

漫天的紫、漫地的蓝

Purple are all over sky and blue are all down to the earth

我在缤纷里驻足

I stopped in these riotous of profusion

人曰年年岁岁花相似

It says that every year flowers are similar

又道是岁岁年年人不同

Every year people are different

我却尤忆过往的年华

Yet, I particularly remember the years of past

我在紫色里欢悦

I was joyful in purple

笑容揉进炫目的蓝

Smiles were rolled into the dazzling blue

你在紫色里低头

You bowed head down in purple

可是那梦幻里的深情

Is that because of the dreamed deep-love

落花有意

The waterside flower pining for love sheds petals

流水无情

While the heartless brook babbles on

带走的，错过的、流殇的

Those were taken away, missed and flowed

故故事事

Stories and stories

留恋的、不甘的、放手的

Nostalgia, unwillingness and the one gave up

还是萦绕在心头

Still obsessed over mind

又是一季蓝花楹

Jacaranda season returns

可是那年的紫、犹如那年的蓝

Is that still purple of that year, just like the blue of that year

你在繁花紫艳里迷朦

You are lost in the brilliant purple of blooming flowers

我将漫天的蓝入诗

I wrote the blue full over the sky into my poems

配一曲高山流水

Match music of High Mountain and Flow Water

弹弹炫炫随云游

Play the stringer / flying with clouds

在紫色里记忆

Remember in purple

在蓝色里忘记

Forget in blue

《车河》

CAR RIVER

老军桥上车河如流

Car river flows on the Anzac Bridge

灯火阑珊处伊人兀自行

The one sitting in the car under the lights dim

收音机里《相见恨晚》

Song "I Wish I Could Have Known You Earlier" in the radio

抑扬的女声在空气中顿挫

The voice of a lady singer cadence in the air

弥漫的清高恰到独好

Scattered rarefied air is just about right

此时的心情

Mood of this moment

彼时的感觉

Feelings of that time

纷纷绕绕的抹不去

One after another around is unable to be erased

忽而热忽而凉的夏

Suddenly hot suddenly cold of the summer

穿梭在异国的灯火车河

Cross over the car river lights on the foreign land

拥堵的路孤独的心

Crowded road, lonely heart

任清风吹散深藏的暗流

Let the clear breeze blow up the deeply hided undercurrent

如车河、如风行

Like the car river, like the walking of wind

不停留、不等待

No stay, no wait

各自的路上默默致意

Greeting silently on the way of self-own

独自安好

Be well alone

《江湖¹⁴忘》

FORGET IN GANGHOOD

记忆滴冰成河

Memories drop ices into river

藏在心底

Hide at the bottom of heart

冷漠是一道闸门

Indifferent is a gole

将汹涌挡在堤外

Stop storms outside of the dam

云淡风轻的江湖

Light cloud soft breeze of Ganghood

波平如镜

Plain like a mirror

一笑泯恩仇

Kindness and hatred is calmed by laughing

风里来、雨里去的杀戮

Wars in wind or in rain

倦了青青、疲了心意

Tired the youth, fatigued the heart

丢盔卸甲的归隐

Hermit by throwing away weapons and armors

成就佛悟禅开

To achieve Buddhist enlightenment and open Zen mind

听水流潺潺

Listen to sound of water

修满腹平淡

Practice simple

晴日赏花开灿然

Appreciate brilliant bloom in sunny days

雨落会飞叶凄清

Experience leaves desolation in rain

纵横百感于此生

Spend this life in fully filled emotions

你走不相送

Would not say goodbye if you go

若来有香茗

If you come there is welcome tea

潮起潮落本自然

Tide up and tide down is natural

隨遇而安

Be peaceful with situation-encountered

不必苛求

No need overcritical

《蓝花楹》

JACARANDA

夕阳下的蓝花楹

A Jacaranda tree under sunset

在风中摇曳

Leaves flying with breeze

帕托河里金光灿烂

Brilliant golden shines in Parramatta river

我用满树的紫色

Hold purple of the whole trees

翩然起舞

I dance lightly

在夏日的午后款款而落

Dropping in a summer afternoon

任凭最后的温柔

Let the last tenderness

许你一地的凌乱

Promise you messy of an entire land

南半球的花开在十月

Jacaranda blooms in October in the southern hemisphere

没有茉莉的馨香

No fragrant like Jasmine

不比玫瑰的娇艳

Not as charm as rose

我只捧一树的爱恋

Only, holds love of the whole tree

倔强在风中

Unbending in wind

用紫色渲染

Rendering with purple

一丛丛、一簇簇

A bush, a rustle

直到荼蘼

Until extravagant

河畔伊人的蓝花楹

Jacaranda of a riverbank beauty

有人说你的花语

It is said that the florid of you is that

在绝望中等待爱情

Waiting for love in forlornness

执着于冷色偏暖的紫

Persistent the purple of cold but be partial of warm

与遥不可及的蓝天回应

Respond to sky too far away to touch

飞鸟掠过你的枝头

Birds flew over your branches

带着白云淡淡的问候

Bring tender greetings of cloud

其实最好的爱情

Actually, the best love

不过是相见不如怀念

Is rather to miss than to meet

Photo by: Zhao Crowley　　　摄影：向昭

《夜色的行板》

ANDANTINO OF NIGHTLINE

有多久没有在午夜的时光里

How long was it ago that didn't in the time of midnight

带上耳机听一首老歌

Put on the earphone to listen an old song

回转的旋律里

In the swing melody

凉风拂面道晚安

Saying good night with the breeze touching face gently

失散的心境

In a lost mood

好似低回的音符

Like the low back music notes

在夜色的行板里渐渐走远

Walk further and further gradually in the nightline andantino

追不回

Unable to chase back

我不知道那些曾经的故事

I don't know the ever-happened stories

是真实还是梦境

Were they real or just dreams

在心间荡漾着的

The one still rippling in heart

还有多少可以久远

How much left can last any longer

我也不知道

Neither, I don't know

可以忘记的偶尔却升腾的

The one forgot but occasionally rising in mind

还有多少的热情可以持续

How much left can persist in enthusiasm

走在一场自导的独角戏里

Walking in a self-directed one-man-show

认真地表演

Performing seriously

自我感动

Self-moving

咿咿呀呀的台词

Babbling the lines

在暗夜里徘徊

Wandering in nightline time

谱一曲夜色的行板

Compose a nightline andantino

ENDNOTES

1   在澳大利亚的悉尼大学有一棵活了八十八年的蓝花楹树。蓝花楹每年在10月中旬到11月初开紫色的花朵,学生们传说如果没有在蓝花楹第一朵花开花之前好好学习,考试就会过不了关,所以在悉尼大学,学生们也将蓝花楹树称为考试树。2016年11月6日这棵树却轰然倒下了,令很多人感到悲伤

There was a jacaranda tree aged 88 years old in the Sydney University in Australia. Every year between the mid of October till the beginning of November, purple flowers will bloom on jacaranda trees. Student in the Sydney University believes that if someone didn't study before the blooming of first flower, he would not be able to pass exams, therefore jacaranda tree was also called "examination tree" in the Sydney University. However, on 6th November 2016, the fallen of this tree make a lot of people feel sad.

2   海子(1964-1989)中国新诗史上最有影响力的诗人之一。原名查海生。1979年15岁时考入北京大学法律系,1982年大学期间开始诗歌创作。1989年3月26日自杀

Haizi (1964-1989), one of Chinese poet with most influence. Original name is Zha Hai Sheng. Entered into the law falcuty of Beijing University when he was 15 years old in 1979. He started to write poems in 1982 during his university time. He commited a suicide on 26th March 1989

3   诗的背景故事来自于希腊神话
塞王,又名阿克罗伊德斯,是西西里海里塞王岛上面容娇美的美人鱼,她的歌声如天籁般让人无法抗拒,凡听过她的歌声的人必会不顾一切的向她所在的岛屿奔去,但最终都会触礁而沉入深海。
奥德修斯 ,希腊神话中的伊萨卡岛王,大英雄。特洛伊战争胜利后他返回故地,有一段征程途径西西里海。他想听塞王的歌声,但又恐被诱惑致死。他便命船员将其用钢锁捆绑在船桅上,其他船员用石蜡封住耳朵。
当奥德修斯听到塞王的歌声时,他痛苦的想要挣脱钢锁投入情海,但最终躲过一劫,安全抵达彼岸。然而不能诱惑奥德修斯的塞王反而深深的地爱上了奥德修斯,最终自己投入大海殉情。意大利人为了纪念这个传说,在那不勒斯城堡为塞王修筑了雕塑,奉若爱情之神。

Background and resource of the poem come from the Greek Mythology: Sirens, another name is Akroyds, she is a good looking mermaid lives at the Siren Island of Sicilian Sea. Her voice is like teana and make people unable to resist. Anyone heard her song would run towards the island she lives without any fear, but they all finaly would run into rocks and fall deeply into the sea.

Odysseus, King of Isaca Island, a big hero in the Greek Mythology. After win the war of troy, he retruned back to his hometown, there was a journey pass by the Sicilian Sea. He wants to listen to Siren's song, but afraid of death by the temptation. He commonded crews tied him on the boat mast with steels, and the other crews blocked their ears with paraffin.

When Odysseus heard sirens' voice, he was so pain and trying to break away the steel lock and throw himself into the love sea, finally he escaped from the catastrophe and arrived to shore. But because of unable to seduce, Siren falled in love to Odysseus, and put herself into the sea and die a martyr. To memory this legend, the Italians build up a status in the castle of Naples for Sirens and worship her as the Love God.

4 孟婆常驻在地狱的奈何桥边。她的职责,是确保所有前往投胎的鬼魂,都不会记得自己的前世和地府中的一切,以免人世的爱恨纠葛。

孟婆在各溪流河畔 采集药草,加上有迷魂作用的忘川河水,熬制成一种汇集酸、甜、苦、辣、咸、涩、腥、冲八味的迷湯,俗称孟婆汤。服用者会立即完全地失去记忆。要过桥离开地府,就必须喝一碗,確定洗去所有過去的记忆后,才可以抵达來生。

Meng Po (Chinese: 孟婆; literally: "Old Lady Meng") is the Lady of Forgetfulness in Chinese mythology.

Meng Po serves in Diyu, the Chinese realm of the dead, in the 10th court. It is her task to ensure that souls who are ready to be reincarnated do not remember their previous life or their time in hell.

To this end she collects herbs from various earthly ponds and streams to make her Five Flavored Tea of Forgetfulness. This is given to each soul to drink before they leave Diyu. The brew induces instant and permanent amnesia, and all memory of other lives is lost.

Having been purged of all previous sins and knowledge, the dead spirit is sent to be reborn in a new earthly incarnation, and the cycle begins again.

Occasionally people are able to avoid drinking the brew, resulting in past life memories surfacing in children

5 黑色七月： 20世纪 80到90年代末，中国高考的时间通常在7月7日到9日三天， 高三毕业生通常把7月份称为黑色七月，一定程度上反应了这个月份对考生们的煎熬。

Black July: in 1980s to the end of 1990s, 7th – 9th of July was Chinese University Entry Exanmination Month. The high school graduateon students called this month as Black July. From a centain degree it reflects the torment of this month to the graduation students.

6 林黛玉是《红楼梦》中的女主角之一。她从小体弱多病，但生性聪慧，极工诗词，所做诗著文笔与意趣俱佳，故有才女之称。 黛玉葬花是小说中的一个经典片段。黛玉最怜惜花，觉得花落以后葬在土里最干净，她为此还写了《葬花词》，以花喻己，是小说中最美的诗词之一。

Lin Daiyu (also spelled Lin Tai-yu, Chinese: 林黛玉; pinyin: Lín Dàiyù) is one of the principal characters of Cao Xucqin's classic Chincsc novel Dream of the Red Chamber. She is portrayed as a well-educated, intelligent, witty and beautiful young woman of physical frailness who is somewhat prone to occasional melancholy. The romance between Daiyu and Jia Baoyu forms one of the main threads of the book. Daiyu buries flowers is a classic chapter in the novel. Daiyu loves flowers, she thought to burry fallen flowers in earth is the cleanest way, she also wrote a poem for this action, it's one of the most beautiful poems in the novel.

7 薛宝钗是《红楼梦 》中的主要人物，男主人公贾宝玉的姨表姐。她体态丰满，品格端芳，才德兼备，性格大度内敛，从小其人品性格被认为是中国传统文化熏陶出的"完美典範"，喜怒哀乐皆有所压抑，不善表达于言表。宝钗之丰腴与黛玉之灵窍，被人普遍认为是中国古典两种类型美女典范，其安分随时之性格与黛玉 "由著性子生活" 的個性亦形成强烈对比

Xue Baochai：simplified Chinese: 薛宝钗; pinyin: Xuē Bāochāi; "Precious Chai", and her surname is a homophone with "Snow") is one of graceful, her attributes complement those of her cousin Lin Daiyu. Indeed, it has been suggested that the two women are complements of one another – each has exactly the attributes of Cao Xueqin's ideal woman which the other lacksthe principal characters in the classic Chinese novel Dream of the Red Chamber. Described as extremely beautiful and socially

8 清明： 一个中国传统的节日，也是最重要的祭祀节日之一，此传统始于周

朝，大约有两千五百多年的历史，1935年中华民国政府明定4月5日为清明节，也称全民扫墓节。

Qing Ming: A traditional public holiday of China, one of the most important memorial festival. It started from Zhou dynasty, has more than 2500 years old. In 1935, government of China Nationalist Party appointed 5rh of April as the Festival of Qing Ming, it's also called Tomb-Sweeping Day, when Chinese traditionally honor the dead.

9 仓央嘉措（藏文：Tshangs-dbyangs-rgya-mtsho1683.03.01－1706.11.15），门巴族，六世达赖喇嘛，法名罗桑仁钦仓央嘉措，西藏历史上著名的诗人、政治人物。

康熙二十二年（1683年）仓央嘉措生于西藏南部门隅纳拉山下宇松地区乌坚林村的一户农奴家庭，父亲扎西丹增，母亲次旺拉姆。家中世代信奉宁玛派佛教。康熙三十六年（1697年）被当时的西藏摄政王第巴·桑结嘉措认定为五世达赖的转世灵童，同年在桑结嘉措的主持下在布达拉宫举行了坐床典礼。康熙四十四年（1705年）被废，据传在康熙四十五年（1706年）的押解途中圆寂。

仓央嘉措是西藏最具代表的民歌诗人，写了很多细腻真挚的诗歌，其中最为经典的是拉萨藏文木刻版《仓央嘉措情歌》

Zangyang Gyatso (3rd Jan 1683 to 15th Nov 1706): Born in Tibet, is the fifth Dalai Lama, a famous poet and politician in Tibet history.

10 泾渭：泾渭是两条河流。泾河水清，渭河水浑，泾河的水流入渭河时，清浊不混。比喻界限清楚或是非分明

Jing Wei River: Jing and Wei are two rivers. Jing river has clear water, Wei river has muddy water. When Jing river joined into Wei river, clear water and muddy water never mixed. Therefore "Jing Wei"was use as a word to describe a clear boundary or right and wrong are very clear.

11 盤古是中国神话中開天闢地的神祇，傳說天地及萬物都由其身軀和器官變化而成，是全世界神靈仙靈和物靈的主神

Pangu (simplified Chinese: 盘古; traditional Chinese: 盤古; pinyin: Páng ǔ; Wade－Giles: P' an-ku) is the first living being and the creator of all in some versions of Chinese mythology.

¹² 女娲，中国上古神话中的创世女神。又称娲皇、女阴娘娘，史记女娲氏，是华夏民族人文先始，是福佑社稷之正神

Nüwa or Nügua is the mother goddess of Chinese mythology, the sister and wife of Fuxi, the emperor-god. She is credited with creating mankind and repairing the Pillar of Heaven. Her reverential name is Wahuang (Chinese: 娲皇; literally: "Empress Wa")

¹³ 中秋节，又称月夕、秋节、仲秋节、八月节、八月会、追月节、玩月节、拜月节、女儿节或团圆节，是流行于中国众多民族与汉字文化圈诸国的传统文化节日，时在农历八月十五；因其恰值三秋之半，故名，也有些地方将中秋节定在八月十六。

中秋节始于唐朝初年，盛行于宋朝，至明清时，已成为与春节齐名的中国传统节日之一。受中华文化的影响，中秋节也是东亚和东南亚一些国家尤其是当地的华人华侨的传统节口。自2008年起中秋节被列为国家法定节假日。2006年5月20日，国务院列入首批国家级非物质文化遗产名录。

中秋节自古便有祭日、赏月、拜月、吃月饼、赏桂花、饮桂花酒等习俗，流传至今，经久不息。中秋节以月之圆兆人之团圆，为寄托思念故乡，思念亲人之情，祈盼丰收、幸福，成为丰富多彩、弥足珍贵的文化遗产。中秋节与端午节、春节、清明节并称为中国四大传统节日。

The Mid-Autumn Festival (also called Moon Festival) is a harvest festival, celebrated by ethnic Chinese and Eastern Asian countries. The festival is held on the 15th day of the 8th month of the lunar calendar with full moon at night, corresponding to late September to early October of the Gregorian calendar with a full moon at night.

Due to ancient China's cultural influence, Mid-Autumn Festival spread to other parts of Asia. Moon cakes have also appeared in western countries as an exotic sweet

¹⁴ 江湖与河流、湖泊并无关系，也不是一个实际存在的场所所，它是指四处流浪、卖艺、卖药的人的一种生活状态。在中国文化中有多重引申含义。指远离朝廷與公家的民间；在许多中国文学中，尤其是武侠小说中，江湖则是侠客们的活动范围；甚至也是黑社会的代称。

Jianghu or jiang hu or 江湖, pronounce similar like Ganghood (lit. "Rivers and lakes") may refer to a community of martial artists in action stories and, more recently, outlaw societies like the Triads.

ABOUT THE AUTHOR

向昭

1972年1月出生于中国陕西西安。祖父曾留学于日本早稻田大学学习陶艺与中国水墨画,自幼生长在教育艺术氛围浓厚的家庭,5岁时第一次在父母任教的学校校刊发表一首描写花园小白花的短诗,受妈妈的鼓励,喜欢用笔记录对生活的感受与思考。中学时参加校园诗社。1996年毕业于西北政法大学国际经济法系后,在陕西财经学院(后合并于西安交通大学)任教。2000年留学澳大利亚麦考瑞大学,获得商法硕士学位,毕业后移民成为澳大利亚公民。现在定居于悉尼,作者保留了用笔记录生活与感受的习惯,经常在微博,微信中发表一些短文,诗歌,游记等。作者喜欢旅游与美食烹饪,至今已经游历了大部分欧国家,以及美国加拿大和东南亚,中国包括香港,台湾等大部分地区,也经常喜欢邀约朋友于家中聚会,烹饪创意美食。作者生活经历丰富,感情强烈。本诗集收录了作者写于2016年11月至2017年11月之间的愈百首中,长度诗歌。

Zhao Crowley:

Born at Xi' an of P.R of China in January 1972, the author grows up from a family with rich educational and artistic atmosphere. Her grandfather has ever been an overseas student study Pottery and Chinese Ink Painting at Waseda University in Japan. At age five, the author published her first short poem at campus magazine at her parents' teaching school, the poem is about a white flower in the campus garden. Encouraged by mother, since then, she likes to record her feelings and things of life by pen. She attended poem group at high school. In 1996 after the author graduated from the North-West University of Politics and Law Science, she became an assistant lecture at the Shannxi Finance Institute (joint with Xi' an Jiaotong University)。 The author came to Australia in 2000 and studied at the Macquarie University, Obtained a master degree of Commercial Law. After the graduation, she immigrated into Australia and became as an Australia citizen. She now lives in Sydney. The author kept her habit to record her life experience and feelings by pen, she published some small articles, poems and travel stories at her blog, social web WeChat etc. She likes travel and cook, until now she traveled most parts of Europe, America and Canada, as well as South-East Asia and most areas in China including Hong Kong and Taiwan. She likes invite friends come to home and cook creative delicious food. The author has rich life experience and has strong feelings about life. This poem collection collect poems she wrote between November 2016 to November 2017 over 100 pieces.

ABOUT THE BOOK

这本诗集包含了 110 首诗。大部分诗写于2016年11月到2017年11月间，为中等到长诗篇幅。这一年的生活给予了作者强烈的感情体验，大部分的感情和移民生活，爱情及人与人之间的关系相关。读着这些诗，你能够感觉到作者表达出的感情，比如爱情，从初次的相见，陷入爱情，直到分离的悲伤。诗中作者表达了欢乐，孤独，悲伤，道义挣扎及其他一些情绪。每一页有一首独立的诗，但整个诗集连贯起来，读者或许会发现一个完整的爱情故事的线索。此诗集或许给你带来人生的思考，有关于找到自我，爱情与道德关系的复杂性，寻找真实自我与生活在社会规则之下的冲突性.每个人的答案或许不同，答案自在每个读者的心中。

This bilingual poem collection contains one hundred and ten poems; most of the poems are in middle-to-long length. It was written by the author from November 2016 to November 2017. During this time, the life experience stirred up the author's strong feelings about immigration life, love, relationship, and others. Reading these poems, you can experience emotions about falling in love from first glance to the sadness of separation or break up. In the poems, the author expressed her feelings of joy, loneliness, sadness, moral struggling, and other emotions. Every page has just one single poem; however, the whole poem collection has a clue to be a love story from beginning to the end. This poem collection may let you think about the life of human being, how to find yourself, the complex feature of love relationship and moral, the conflict of finding your real self, and the life under social rules. Everyone's thought may be different, but the answer is in your heart.

Printed and bound by PG in the USA